BLACK LEGISLATORS

By Robert T. Perry

San Francisco, California
1977

Published in 1976 by

R AND E RESEARCH ASSOCIATES
4843 Mission Street, San Francisco 94112
18581 McFarland Avenue, Saratoga, California 95070

Publishers and Distributors of Ethnic Studies

Library of Congress Card Catalog Number

75-5333

ISBN

0-88247-389-1

Acknowledgements

Words which adequately express a feeling of deep gratitude and sincere appreciation are missing from Webster's catalog of the English vocabulary. This deficiency will hopefully be recognized by those persons acknowledged in the following paragraphs. Without their collective counsel, assistance and patience any accomplishment related to this study would have been considerably more difficult, if not completely impossible.

The following pages represent a slightly modified version of a Ph.D. dissertation written at the University of Missouri-Columbia under the advisement and guidance of Dr. Robert Karsch. His suggestions were most helpful and added considerably to the writing of this manuscript. Comments and assistance from Dr. Gregory Casey who read the dissertation were beneficial in improving the final product. Other faculty members who contributed to my education and who willingly offered their counsel in the preparation of this study include Dr. Lloyd Wells, Dr. Anthony Dworkin, Dr. David Wood and Dr. Dean Yarwood.

Vital to the data reported and analyzed in this study were the thirteen black legislators in the Missouri House of Representatives during the 1969-70 session. Their willingness to share their time and insights with me greatly facilitated the research effort. I am greatly indebted to those individuals who provided the aggregate for this study, the Honorables Johnie S. Aiken, J.B. "Jet" Banks, DeVerne Calloway, Russell Goward, Harold Holliday, Herman Johnson, Leon Jordon, Leroy Malcolm, Franklin Payne, Nathaniel (Nat) Rivers, Henry Ross, James Troupe and Fred Williams.

My thanks to the Department of Political Science of the University of Missouri for providing financial assistance for the project. Also, my appreciation to Dr. Roy Gruenewald and the Department of Political Science at Ball State University for their compassion with my needs in the final preparation stages. The dedication of Ms. Jill Alcorn, Ms. Maureen Hughes, Mrs. Bernice Nesper, and Mrs. Madonna Checkeye in the task of typing various drafts has been greatly appreciated.

Vital to any pursuit of this magnitude is the devotion and encouragement which comes from one's family. My wife, Jane, has served as typist, supporter, critic and confidant. Without her understanding and devotion this goal would not have been achieved. My son, Tod, provided assistance as well as periodic prodding. His willingness to make sacrifices has made it easier to complete the task. My son, Jay, whose patience in joining our family was greatly appreciated. My parents, Dr. and Mrs. Thomas A. Perry, are appreciated for their continued encouragement and confidence. A special thanks to my father who took time to lend considerable editorial advice. Also, my appreciation to Mrs. Laurie Massie for her editorial assistance. The appropriate words have yet to be invented which would express my gratitude to Joe and Joyce Weiker for their assistance and for just being there.

Needless to say, whatever faults might be found with the following pages rests solely at my feet.

iii

TABLE OF CONTENTS

TABLE OF CONTENTS (Continued)

Chapter

Chapter

LIST OF TABLES

LIST OF TABLES (Continued)

LIST OF TABLES (Continued)

LIST OF FIGURES

CHAPTER I

INTRODUCTION

It has been estimated that in 1960 thirty-six Negroes served as state legislators in the United States.[1] In 1970 one hundred and sixty-eight blacks were elected to membership in state legislatures.[2] This more than seven-fold ratio of increased participation by blacks in the state legislative processes provides the basis for this study. As access to state deliberative bodies increases for blacks, it is necessary to raise several questions about the Negro legislator and his role in the legislative process. The research reported in the following pages is dedicated to asking some of those questions and, as a result, providing a clearer understanding of the Negro solon and his position in a state legislature.

A foundation for the research reported in this manuscript will be laid in this chapter. Commencing with the establishment of the utility and the need for this project, it is necessary to review the literature bordering on the concerns of this study. Once the gap in the literature has been demonstrated, the specific study and its suppositions can be described. It is at this point that the nexus of this research and its relevance to knowledge in the field of political science can be justified. Data collection techniques used in this study will be explained in a subsequent section. The final section will be devoted to a description of the methodological framework used in the study.

Concerns in the Literature

Ethnic groups

In the past decade a substantial amount of literature has been produced on the subject of ethnic groups in the American society. Where the orientation has been on the general role of ethnicity, proportionately the blacks have received the most attention. This trend can largely be explained by the overall societal focus on black problems in the past decade and a half. National government decisions coupled with the growth and activism of the civil rights movement have provided the impetus for scholarly activity.

Ethnic groups have been defined as "those who conceive of themselves as being alike by virtue of common ancestry, real or fictitious, and who are so regarded by others."[3] Unequivocally, American Negroes are included within the boundaries of this definition. The relationship

1

of ethnicity to American politics has been the central theme in several studies. Most prominent of these have been the writings of Robert Dahl, Raymond Wolfinger, and Michael Parenti. Dahl developed a continuum of political assimilation which proposed that ethnicity would recede as a political variable. More important than his expectation of complete assimilation, however, was the fact that ethnicity has been and continues to be a component of American political behavior.[4] Dahl wrote:

> . . . the very fact that the politician exploited ethnic unities and distinctions helped to fortify and maintain--at times perhaps even to create--feelings of ethnic difference among voters of otherwise similar social and economic circumstances. The politicians acted out a self-fulfilling prophecy; by treating ethnic distinctions as fundamental in politics, they made them fundamental.[5]

Wolfinger sustained Dahl's conclusions in New Haven by arguing that the political salience and effects of ethnicity will remain even when assimilation occurs.[6] Parenti while arguing that Dahl and Wolfinger had proposed the wrong question, that of assimilation, sustained their general conclusion that ethnicity remains a prominent political variable.[7]

Whereas disagreements exist among authors on the reasons for and the degree of ethnic group political salience, the authors agree that it does exist and that it does play a major role in politics. Blacks as a separate and identifiable entity within the American political system can be justified on the grounds that Negroes are defined as one of several ethnic groups and that ethnicity is a viable component of the system. This foundation has been concretely established in the literature.

A complete understanding of political behavior cannot be gained without some awareness of the environmental conditions which serve as a premise for such activity. Several descriptions of the black community in America have been published which not only describe the conditions of black America today, but also provide a basis for understanding the psychological attitudes among persons of the Negro race. Attitudes held by blacks toward the political system are affected by two basic inter-related ingredients, the historical situation of Negroes in America and the circumstances which surround their life in contemporary society. The historical repression of blacks politically, as well as socially and economically, has been well documented.[8] The past relegation of blacks to inferior societal positions has produced a multitude of problems in the present black community: poverty, high crime rates, unemployment, broken homes, low educational achievement, etc. . . .[9] Black attitudes of alienation and hostility toward the American political system have resulted from these environmental factors.[10]

Whereas patterns and conditions of life are essential to the comprehension of a group's role within a political system, the focus of this project is directed at the political patterns and conditions of the black community. The literature on Negro participation in the American political system has been concentrated around several themes.

The exclusion of blacks from political participation has received much attention.[11] Although recent statistics have shown increases in black participation, it continues to be a major topic for researchers.[12] When permitted to participate, blacks have demonstrated their willingness by engaging in a wide range of political activities rather than restricting themselves to the most elementary activity of voting.[13]

As a result of increased opportunities for political participation, the impact that blacks have on political institutions has been examined. Studies of impact have shown that when group cohesion is exhibited in voting, the greatest impacts are made on public issues related to the distribution of public services, particularly when referendum elections are held.[14] Negro influence tends to be greatest when blacks constitute a majority of the voting population or when they are only small minorities within the voting electorate.[15] In situations where they are large minorities, but not a majority, the impact lessens as a result of race salience which produces white resistance.[16]

The strategy utilized in the black community to maximize their political position has been investigated and reported from a number of perspectives. It has been argued that blacks should refrain from becoming partners in coalitions with non-blacks, especially if blacks are not accepted as full and equal partners and if the achievement of black goals is not guaranteed.[17] Since blacks are not generally a majority of the electorate in most political sub-systems, it is usually necessary for the blacks to enter into some type of coalition in order to obtain any status within, or demands from the political institutions. The type of coalition and the role of the black political organization can vary greatly. Wilson argues that it is the style of politics within the different communities which will determine the strategy style that will be most beneficial to blacks.[18] For instance, the blacks may be able to establish an independent organization which has no permanent alliances with non-black elements of the political community in order to obtain any political benefits.[20]

At the national level blacks have coalesced with the Democratic Party since the 1930's.[21] The significance of the Negro element of the Democratic Party has been illustrated by Axelrod's recent study where he argued that the blacks contributed one fifth of the national vote for the party in 1968.[22] Although blacks have generally identified with one of the two dominant political parties since the Civil War era, there have been repeated attempts to draw the blacks away from those parties. Walton's study of third parties in the United States shows the great variety of movements which made overtures to the black community.[23] Of the non-black third parties, the ideological or doctrinaire type has consistently attempted to lure the blacks into its fold, as documented by Record's report on the Communist Party.[24] The use of the third party movement as a political strategy for blacks has had only limited success.[25]

Typologies of black leadership have been a common theme in the literature on black politics.[26] The studies have commonly focused on general leadership roles, rather than the formal political leadership in the black community. Where each study develops a spectrum ranging from traditional or conservative to liberal or militant, a common consensus has been that those blacks who occupy positions of formal authority fall into the moderate type. There are, however, some exceptions to the general pattern. The moderate style of leadership represents a leader who strives to minimize racial conflict in his community while at the same time seeking gradual integration. A moderate would prefer bargaining and negotiation to mass action or extra-legal strategies.

The literature on blacks who hold leadership positions within the political system is limited. Some general descriptions have been offered,[27] but most of the material available is limited to statements of attitudes and goals.[28] Reference to the performance by blacks who occupy positions within political institutions is almost non-existent.[29]

Legislatures

Although there is a scarcity of literature on black legislative politics, the volume of literature on legislatures is quite large. Legislative systems and their components have been described and analyzed on a broad spectrum. The field ranges from studies of the National Congress to narrower one-unit investigations within the framework of the American sub-national systems. Not only has the breadth of the legislative process on a political system unit basis been intensively examined, but there is also abundant literature on the integral parts of the legislative systems.

State legislative systems have been described in several studies.[30] These studies will serve continually as references to the general nature of state legislatures. There are also more prominent and related specialized studies of legislative systems, particularly on state systems. These studies may be classified under four topics: categoric legislative groups, personal characteristics of legislators, recruitment of legislators, and the legislative structures.

Categoric groups--the classification of legislators on the basis of some common denominator shared by all of the group's members--[31] have served as the orientation of several studies. Although the category used in this study, race, has hitherto received scant attention, other group classifications such as political party affiliation,[32] geographical locations of constituencies,[33] constituency types,[34] and personal characteristics[35] have been employed. Ethnicity has served as a basis for categoric classification in only one, now outdated, legislative study.[36]

Personal characteristics of legislators, as these are transmitted by the political socialization process, have received much attention in research related to legislative systems. Variables of political socialization commonly described are those of family background, occupation,

4

education, social status, and residential mobility.[37] Variables related to a legislator's initial interest in politics and his pre-legislative political experience have received increasing attention in the literature.[38] The four-state study by Wahlke and others on role perceptions was a major contribution to the literature on political socialization of state legislators.[39]

The process of selecting state legislators has been described from several perspectives. Apportionment of legislative districts received considerable attention in the 1960's.[40] Selgiman's study in Oregon provides an understanding of the various forces which are involved in candidate selection.[41] The election process has been reviewed for both primary and general elections, particularly with regard to party competitiveness.[42]

The internal legislative processes and organization have been given considerable attention by political scientists. Most of these studies are limited to examinations of particular state legislatures. Politics and practices of state legislatures have been a common orientation.[43] Leadership roles have received limited attention.[44] Several studies have focused on the role of committees in state legislatures.[45]

More important to this study is the existence of literature on the Missouri state legislature. Much of the attention has been oriented to descriptive explanations of legislators' backgrounds.[46] Young's manuscript described the legislative political parties in the mid-fifties.[47] The urban-rural alignments within the legislature were given attention in Derge's study.[48] Basic descriptions of the organization and structure can be found in Karsch's general textbook on Missouri.[49] The committee system in the Missouri General Assembly is discussed by Karsch in The Standing Committees in the Missouri General Assembly.[50]

The Study

Need for the study

The purpose of any research is to provide enlightenment on a subject which has, heretofore, been unattended or to provide a deeper understanding of those topics which have been investigated by previous studies. This project has as its purpose the furtherance of knowledge on the political behavior of an ethnic group in American state politics. Its validity with reference to the purpose of research must be reviewed.

Illustrated by the review of literature in the discipline of political science, a void exists in research related to the specific topic of this study. It is true that considerable attention has focused on ethnic political behavior, particularly in the past decade; and legislative processes and behaviors have also received considerable research attention. Although the literature is abundant on both topics, no attempt has been made to relate categoric group behavior in the legislature to ethnicity in the officialdom of government. The premise

upon which this study is founded is the utility of having such an understanding of legislators who share a common ancestral heritage--in this
case, the Negro.

What justification can there be for the realization of this
desire to bridge this gap in the research? What utility is there in
having some knowledge of Negro legislators? Three reasons compel the
belief that there is a need to bridge the literature gap and that a
utility does exist for this study.

First, most evident is the fact that Negroes have been elected
to legislative bodies, particularly state legislatures, in increasing
numbers in the past decade. As Negro legislators are elected in
increasing numbers, the proportion of black legislators within the
legislative bodies has increased. From a numerical perspective, as
the proportion of black members increases, black power or influence
potential within the legislative chamber increases. As a collective
group the blacks now hold more power or influence potential in state
legislative bodies than they did in past periods. As a result, blacks
have become an increasingly important sub-unit of the legislative
system.

Secondly, one of the most dominant domestic issues of the 1960's
was civil rights. Two results of the civil rights movement seem pertinent as the basis for this study. First, the movement manifested the
consciousness of blacks that they were not proportionally represented
in the political system. Secondly, the movement articulated a desire
for alterations in public policies related to racial concerns. The
combination of these two phenomena required legislative structures to
be more cognizant of the black community needs. As delegates from the
Negro communities,[51] the Negro representatives would, seemingly, assume
the responsibility for translating constituency inputs into desired
public policy. The consciousness of black concerns manifested by the
civil rights movement placed the Negro representative in a position of
being not simply a legislator, but a Negro legislator.

Thirdly, the study has merit as an indicator of the societal
relations between racial groups. Whereas legal stratification between
black and white America is slowly becoming non-existent, there do remain
some social and attitude barriers to group assimilation. The extent of
black integration into the legislative body may provide some mirror or
indicator of the broader political culture.

Boundaries of the study

In order to fulfill the purposes of this project, the most
important consideration was the selection of the specific legislature
to be studied. The House of Representatives for the 75th Missouri
General Assembly was selected. Its selection was based upon several
criteria which were pertinent to this research. First, the Missouri
House was accessible. Secondly, the Missouri House provided a unit for
research which was manageable. Although a broader study, a comparison
of several state legislatures or one which would consider the topic over

a period of several sessions, might have been more desirable and meaning-ful, the manageable nature of the Missouri House was a vital consideration, particularly when referring to the factors of accessibility. A third criterion derives from the nature of black representation in the Missouri House in 1969. In 1969 the Missouri House had the largest delegation of black members of any single state legislative chamber in the United States.[52] Also in 1969, there were only three state legislative chambers which had greater proportions of blacks in their membership than the Missouri House.[53] Therefore, from both a raw numerical and a proportional ratio of membership basis, the Missouri House possessed characteristics which made it desirable for an initial study of black legislators.

To restate, the boundaries of this study are limited to: one state, Missouri; one legislative chamber, the House of Representatives; and one legislative session, the regular session of the 75th General Assembly which met from January 8, 1969 to July 15, 1969. As a result, the findings or conclusions drawn from this research are limited. They should, however, provide basic hypotheses or springboards for more com-prehensive studies of ethnic lawmakers.

Two additional limitations or boundaries need to be mentioned. First, this is a study of collective, rather than individual, behavior. The findings apply only to the generalized categoric group and not to the individuals who compose the collective. Secondly, this was not undertaken to provide normative perceptions on the nature of black representatives. Rather, it is a description of their legislative behavior on the basis of such information as it was possible to gather.

A Basic Presupposition

The study undertaken in this research was based upon the general premise that those members of a deliberative body who possess common ancestral characteristics that are atypical of the dominant society, and that serve as a basis for the stratification of a society's member-ship, will exhibit attitudes and behavior patterns which reflect their uniqueness. From this foundation it is expected that the shared char-acteristic, in this case race, will be a salient and vital determinant in the legislative activities of the designated group. Not only will the in-group members, those who share the common denominator or char-acteristic, perceive their sameness as a component of their legislative behavior patterns, but also the dominant elements of the legislative body will refer to this distinction in their relations and interactions with the subordinate ethnic group.

Literature on race relations in the United States has shared the central theme that the American Negro has been and remains in a subordinate and inferior position in the stratified American society, politically, as well as socially and economically.[54] The task designed for this research has as its focus two interrelated themes. First, there is an examination of the black representatives in the House to determine if their shared racial characteristic did affect their legis-lative behaviors and attitudes. Secondly, there is an attempt to determine if race was utilized as a mechanism to differentiate among the chamber's membership within the internal operation of the legislature. It may be hypothesized that assimilation is no more likely to take place in a collective of society's representatives than it is to occur in the greater society, if society, in general, retains its desire to restrict its primary associations and to prohibit complete interaction on the basis of some ascribed characteristic which results in some group being relegated to a subordinate position. To this general hypothesis, and its components, the following study is directed for an increased understanding of the black legislator.

Data Collection

In researching the different components of this study, data was collected from several sources. The basic data types correspond to the three sources from which the information was gathered.

First, information was collected from the individuals who were members of the categoric group under study. Each black representative was requested to complete a questionnaire designed to obtain basic biographical and attitudinal information. In addition, personal interviews were conducted with twelve of the black representatives.[55]

The second type of data utilized in this study came from government records and publications. Data related to personal characteristics of the legislators and election statistics came from the Official Manual State of Missouri.[56] Information on the internal operations and actions of the House was taken from the House Journal.[57]

The third basic resource used was newspapers. The newspapers were used as a supplement to information collected from the first two basic sources. They were most helpful in providing general information about the political situation in the black communities. In using newspapers an emphasis was placed upon the Negro press.[58]

Methodological Framework

A systematic and orderly procedure is needed for both the investigation and reporting of research if its purpose is to intelligibly increase man's understanding. In subscribing to those criteria, it is necessary that some general framework be constructed. The usefulness of any particular framework will depend upon its practicality as a nexus between research components. Adopted for this project was a framework that utilizes elements from the group and systems approaches.

The group approach to politics had its inception in the writings of Arthur Bentley.[59] Since Bentley's development of the group approach, it has received considerable attention in the discipline. The basis for the use of the group concept is the assumption that society is structured on associational relationships.[60] A group in its broadest form may be defined as "any collection of individuals who have some characteristic

in common."[61] Truman, however, concluded that the existence of interaction between the individuals forming the group was a proper addition
to the definition.[62] The definition, even with the added element of
interaction, is considerably broad in its scope. Within the boundaries
of the definition are two distinctively different types of groups
according to the regulation of the groups' activities and interaction
patterns. Latham made this distinction between conscious groups and
organized groups. The former he defines as those groups where a
"community sense exists but which has not become organized."[63] The
latter are those groups which have "established an objective and formal
apparatus."[64] This study is concerned with Latham's conscious group
type. A better description of this group type can be found in discussion
by Alan Fiellin.[65] Fiellin uses the terminology of "informal" and
"formal" groups to make the distinction on the basis of the groups'
structural relationships. An informal group is "an identifiable, self-
conscious, relatively stable unit of interacting members whose relationships are not officially prescribed by statutes and rules."[66] The formal
group would have the same characteristics, except it would be governed
by some prescribed statutes or roles.[67]

This research utilizes Fiellin's definition of an informal group.
The black legislators are an identifiable collective; they are conscious
of their common characteristics, and the membership is stable according
to the common denominator which defines the group's membership. These
group characteristics can be related to the earlier definition of an
ethnic group: "those who conceive of themselves as being alike by virtue
of common ancestry, real or fictitious, and who are so regarded by
others."[68] Thus, the black House members can be defined as a group.
Their classification as an informal group was based upon the premise
that there were no prescribed rules which regulated the group's
activities or relationships. No external rules and likewise no internal
regulating apparatus existed to govern the group during the period
studied.

The group approach provides a mechanism for concentrating
attention on an associational element of the political system. Whereas
the group approach is utilized for the purpose of focusing attention
on one such group, it is not the purpose of this research to relate the
specified group to the whole political system. To the contrary, the
project is limited to a sub-unit of the broad political system, a state
political system. Furthermore, it is oriented to a further sub-division
of the state's political system, the legislative system. Within the
state legislative system, the attention narrows to the sub-system of
one legislative chamber. The use of the group approach within the
framework of a legislative system has been substantiated by Truman's
work on the National Congress. Truman argued, "A legislative body has
its own group life, sometimes as a unit, perhaps more often as a
collection of sub-groups or cliques."[69] It is within the confines of
the above discussion that this project proposes to use the group approach
within a single legislative chamber.

Where the group approach permits research to concentrate its
efforts on an identifiable association or collective, it is not sufficient

within itself to provide a framework for understanding the phenomena in this research. In order to provide with clarity an understanding of the group's behavior, the systems approach was modified.

A political system is distinguished from other social systems by its legitimate use of coercive authority. Easton refers to this as the "authoritative allocation of values."[70] The political system can be said to be all those interrelated structures and processes which interact to authoritatively allocate values. Implicit in the definition is the relatedness of those components which compose the system. A system also implies that a boundary exists. Those activities which are political are within the political system and those activities which are not related to the political system are seen as outside the boundary. A sub-unit of the broader political system is those activities which perform the rule-making function for the system. This study will perceive the legislature as a system within itself: a collective of activities related to the general system's lawmaking function which interacts for the authoritative allocation of values, which has several interacting components and which is restricted by some boundary.

This project, however, is not directly concerned with all those activities which take place in the performance of the legislative function. The concern to which this project is addressed are those activities and interactions of the black representatives, as a group, as they take place within the legislative system. A modified systems model with several components is used to guide this discussion.

The first component of the model is the environment from which the black solons have emerged.[71] To understand attitude and behavior patterns, it is helpful to know first something about those characteristics which provide the group's situation within the polity. Chapter Two is devoted to a description of environmental factors which may serve as a foundation for political activity. Included are characteristics of class status, residency, age, education, occupation, and sex. In addition, the legislator's commitments to his district and his affiliation with ethnic or racial organizations are presented.

Two other components of the model are discussed in Chapter Three.[72] Initial attention is given to the process of political socialization. This concern is presented as the acquisition of interest in the political system and those related factors which premised the individual's decision to seek a position within the legislative system. The socialization of an individual to the extent that there is a desire to seek office is necessary if the individual is to become involved in the next component, the electoral process. In the latter portions of the chapter, attention is devoted to those factors related to the selection of the individual for membership in the legislative system. Whereas political socialization, the acquiring of all political attitudes, has broader implications than those used in this project, it is restricted in this project to those attitudes related to the recruitment of legislators. Political socialization and the selection process are placed under the umbrella, "recruitment", in this study.

10

Political culture has been defined as those attitudes, beliefs, and values held by individuals toward the political system.[73] It is this component of the model to which attention is given in Chapter Four. Attitudes or perceptions held by the black assemblyman are presented within four areas which were believed to relate to their activities within the legislative system. Since racial stratification has been both a legal phenomenon as well as a social custom in parts of the United States, the attitudes possessed by blacks on racial matters were seen as salient to their role as lawmakers. As a result of the racial composition of their constituency, the black representatives' beliefs as to the Negro community's concerns on policy outputs were also included. Perceptions on the role of blacks in the political system serve as the third area considered. A fourth area relates to the black representative's perceptions of his relations with his constituency.

The first three components of the model--environment, recruitment, and attitudes--deal with phenomena that affect interactions and activities within the legislative system, but are not model components which describe the patterns of behavior that occur within the intimate confines of the legislature and its membership. The following three parts of the model are intended to perform that function.

Structures exist within the legislative system to promote the regularity of activities that occur.[74] In essence there is some organizational mechanism which coordinates the activities of the system's membership. Chapter Five is devoted to this component, organized structure. The black collective in the legislature was examined with regard to its status in the organizational structure of the chamber. The relationship of black representatives with leadership roles is given attention in the first section. The process by which the legislative task is divided, the committee system, provides the basis for the second part of the chapter.

The processes by which policy inputs are or are not converted into policy outputs have been referred to as the conversion function.[75] In Chapter Six attention is given to the legislative process in converting policy inputs initiated within the legislative framework by the black representatives. Inputs from the Negro assemblymen, as defined by the legislative items they sponsored or jointly-sponsored, are examined for purposes of locating the type of demands placed upon the House. The success of the legislative input in being converted into policy outputs is discussed in a second section. Perceptions of the black group on desirable policy inputs and successes in conversion are the focus in a third section.

The phenomenon of performance by the system, the way the system carries out its tasks, has been referred to as system capability.[76] The model utilized here has a modified capability function to signify how blacks performed within the larger legislative system. This serves as the final component of the model for this study. Under the capability component attention is centered on voting behavior of the Negro solons in the House: black group cohesion on roll-call voting, black voting

11

deviation from the norms established by comparable legislators, and black group support for the political party on roll-call votes. A second section is devoted to the impact of black voting patterns on legislative decisions. A final sub-area is the performance of the black membership in the legislative voting process. These components provide a basis for an understanding of the group's performance within the legislative system.

Notes

[1]Revolution in Civil Rights (3rd ed.; Washington: Congressional Quarterly, Inc., 1967), p. 120.

[2]The Black Politician (Summer, 1970), p. 20, cited by Hanes Walton, Jr., Black Politics (New York: J. B. Lippincott Company, 1972), p. 199. Also, National Roster of Black Elected Officials (Washington: Metropolitan Applied Research Center, Inc., 1970).

[3]Tamotsu Shibutani and Kian M. Kwan, Ethnic Stratification (New York: Macmillan Company, 1965), p. 47.

[4]A discussion on assimilation theory is offered by Milton M. Gordon, "Assimilation in America: Theory and Reality," Daedalus, XC (Spring, 1961), 263-285; and by his Assimilation in American Life (New York: Oxford University Press, 1964).

[5]Robert A. Dahl, Who Governs? Democracy and Power in an American City (New Haven: Yale University Press, 1961), p. 54.

[6]Raymond E. Wolfinger, "The Development and Persistence of Ethnic Voting," American Political Science Review, LIX (December, 1965), pp. 896-908.

[7]Michael Parenti, "Ethnic Politics and the Persistence of Ethnic Identification," American Political Science Review, LXI (September, 1967), 717-726.

[8]Extensive discussions on this point can be found in John Hope Franklin, "The Two Worlds of Race: A Historical View," Daedalus, XCIV (Fall, 1965), 899-920; and Gunnar Myrdal, An American Dilemma (2nd ed.; New York: Harper and Row, 1962).

[9]See, Kenneth Clark, Dark Ghetto (New York: Harper and Row, 1967); St. Clair Drake and Horace Cayton, Black Metropolis (New York: Harcourt, Brace and World, Inc., 1965); Charles E. Silberman, Crisis in Black and White (New York: Random House, Inc., 1964); and Nathan Glazer (Cambridge, Mass.: The M.I.T. Press, 1963), chapter 2.

[10]Discussions on negative attitudes can be located in Clark, op. cit.; and Charles S. Bullock, III, and Harrell R. Rogers, Jr. (eds.), Black Political Attitudes (Chicago: Markham Publishing Company, 1972).

[11]The best discussions on this point can be found in John H. Fenton and Kenneth W. Vines, "Negro Registration in Louisiana," American Political Science Review, LI (September, 1957), 704-713; Walton, op. cit., chapter 3; and Donald R. Matthews and James W. Prothro, Negroes and the New Southern Politics (New York: Harcourt, Brace and World, Inc., 1966), chapter 1.

[12]Walton, op. cit., p. 44.

[13]Matthews and Prothro, op. cit., p. 55.

[14]William R. Keech, The Impact of Negro Voting (Chicago: Rand McNally and Company, 1968), pp. 95-98.

[15]Ibid., pp. 101-102.

[16]Keech, loc. cit.; and Donald R. Matthews and James W. Prothro, "Social and Economic Factors and Negro Voter Registration in the South," American Political Science Review, LVII (March, 1963), p. 29.

[17]Stokely Carmichael and Charles V. Hamilton, Black Power: The Politics of Liberation in America (New York: Vintage Books, 1967), pp. 77-81.

[18]James Q. Wilson, "Two Negro Politicians: An Interpretation," Midwest Journal of Political Science, IV (November, 1960), 360-369; and James Q. Wilson, "The Negro in Politics," Daedalus, XCIV (Fall, 1965), 949-973.

[19]Discussions on the independent style of politics can be found in Wilson, "Two Negro Politicians," op. cit.; and Harry Holloway, "Negro Political Strategy: Coalition or Independent Power Politics," Social Science Quarterly, XLIX (December, 1968), 534-547. Wilson describes the Adam Clayton Powell organization in New York. Holloway's independent organization is in Memphis.

[20]Wilson, "Two Negro Politicians," op. cit.; and Holloway, op. cit. Holloway discusses the alliances in Houston and Atlanta. The Dawson organization in Chicago is described by Wilson.

[21]Discussions on the Negro affiliation with the Democratic Party are found in Walton, op. cit., chapter 7; and Harold F. Gosnell, Negro Politicians: The Rise of Negro Politicians in Chicago (Chicago: Phoenix Press, 1966), pp. 23-36.

[22]Robert Axelrod, "Where the Votes Come From: An Analysis of Electoral Coalitions, 1952-1968," American Political Science Review, LXVI (March, 1972), pp. 11-20.

[23]Hanes Walton, Jr., The Negro in Third Party Politics, (Philadelphia: Dorrance and Company, 1969).

[24]Wilson Record, The Negro and the Communist Party (Durham: University of North Carolina Press, 1951).

[25]The only recent black third party movement accorded much success has been the Mississippi Freedom Democratic Party. See Walton, Black Politics, op. cit., pp. 124-125.

[26]Everett Carll Ladd, Jr., Negro Political Leadership in the South (New York: Cornell University Press, 1966), chapter 4; Matthews and Prothro, Negroes and the New Southern Politics, op. cit., pp. 191-195; and James Q. Wilson, Negro Politics: The Search for Leadership (New York: The Free Press, 1960), chapter 8.

[27]Mack H. Jones, "Black Officeholders in Local Governments of the South," (unpublished paper presented at the Southern Political Science Association meeting, November, 1970); and Walton, Black Politics, op. cit., pp. 188-202.

[28]An example of this type can be found in Kenneth B. Clark, Julian Bond, and Richard G. Hatcher, The Black Man in American Politics (Washington: Metropolitan Applied Research Center, Inc., 1969); and Mervyn M. Dymally (ed.), The Black Politician: His Struggle for Power (Belmont, California: Duxbury Press, 1971).

[29]The best reference is Wilson's "Two Politicians," op. cit. An historical account of black legislators in Texas can be found in J. Mason Brewer, Negro Legislators of Texas (New York: Jenkins Publishing Company, 1970).

[30]Wilder Crane, Jr., and Meredith W. Watts, Jr., State Legislative Systems (Englewood Cliffs, N.J.: Prentice-Hall, Inc., 1968); Alexander Heard (ed.), State Legislatures in American Politics (Englewood Cliffs, N.J.: Prentice-Hall, Inc., 1966); Malcolm E. Jewell, The State Legislature (2nd ed.; New York: Random House, 1969); Malcolm E. Jewell and Samuel C. Patterson, The Legislative Process in the United States (New York: Random House, 1966); William J. Keefe and Morris S. Ogul, The American Legislative Process (Englewood Cliffs, N.J.: Prentice-Hall, Inc., 1964).

[31]Lee F. Anderson, Meredith W. Watts, Jr., and Allen R. Wilcox, Legislative Roll-Call Analysis (Evanston: Northwestern University Press, 1966), p. 29.

[32]Malcolm E. Jewell, "Party Voting in American State Legislatures," American Political Science Review, XLIX (September, 1955), 773-791; William J. Keefe, "Comparative Study of the Role of Political Parties," Western Political Quarterly, IX (September, 1956), 726-742; Frank J. Sorauf, Party and Representation: Legislative Politics in Pennsylvania (New York: Atherton Press, 1963).

[33]David R. Derge, "Metropolitan and Outstate Alignments in Illinois and Missouri Legislative Delegations," American Political Science Review, LII (December, 1958), 1051-1065; Alan Fiellan, "The Functions of Informal Groups in Legislative Institutions," Journal of Politics, XXIV (February, 1962), 72-91; David B. Truman, The Congressional Party (New York: John Wiley and Sons, Inc., 1959).

[34]Lewis A. Froman, Jr., Congressmen and Their Constituencies (Chicago: Rand McNally and Company, 1963); Duncan MacRae, Jr., "The Relation Between Roll-Call Votes and Constituencies in the Massachusetts House of Representatives," American Political Science Review, XLVI (December, 1952), 1046-1055.

[35]David R. Derge, "The Lawyer as Decision-Maker in the American State Legislature," Journal of Politics, XXI (August, 1959), pp. 408-433; Duncan MacRae, Jr., and Edith K. MacRae, "Legislators' Social Status and Their Votes," American Journal of Sociology, LXVI (May, 1961), 599-603.

[36]John C. Russell, "Racial Groups in the New Mexico Legislature," The Annals (January, 1938), 625-638.

[37]The most prominent of these studies on state legislators are Leon D. Epstein, Politics in Wisconsin (Madison: The University of Wisconsin Press, 1958), chapter 6; Sorauf, op. cit., chapter 4; and John C. Wahlke, et al., The Legislative System (New York: John Wiley and Sons, Inc., 1962), pp. 486-491.

[38]See James David Barber, The Lawmakers (New Haven: Yale University Press, 1965); and Wahlke, et al., op. cit., chapters 4 and 5.

[39]Wahlke, et al., op. cit.

[40]See Gordon E. Baker, The Reapportionment Revolution (New York: Random House, 1966); and Paul T. David and Ralph Eisenbury, State Legislative Districting (Chicago: Public Administration Service, 1962).

[41]Lester G. Selgiman, "Political Recruitment and Party Structure," American Political Science Review, LV (March, 1961), 77-86.

[42]See V. O. Key, Jr., American State Politics (New York: Alfred A. Knopf, Inc., 1956), particularly chapter 6; and Frank J. Sorauf, Party Politics in America (Boston: Little, Brown and Company, 1968).

[43]William Buchanan, Legislative Partisanship: The Deviant Case of California (Berkeley: University of California Press, 1963); Duane Lockard, New England State Politics (Princeton, N.J.: Princeton University Press, 1959); Sorauf, Party and Representation, op. cit.; and Gilbert Y. Steiner and Samuel K. Gove, Legislative Politics in Illinois (Urbana: University of Illinois Press, 1960).

[44] The only work on states of any major significance is the now outdated study, Eugene C. Lee, _The Presiding Officer and the Rules Committee in Legislatures of the United States_ (Berkeley: Bureau of Public Administration, University of California, 1952).

[45] Loren P. Beth and William C. Harvard, "Committee Stacking and Political Power in Florida," _Journal of Politics_, XXIII (February, 1961), 57-83; Robert F. Karsch, _The Standing Committees of the Missouri General Assembly_ (Columbia, Missouri: Bureau of Government Research of the University of Missouri, 1959); and Dean E. Mann, "The Legislative Committee System in Arizona," _Western Political Quarterly_, XIV (December, 1961), 925-941.

[46] Don F. Hadwiger, "Representation in the Missouri General Assembly," _Missouri Law Review_, XXII (April, 1959), 178-195; and David A. Leuthold, _The Missouri Legislature: A Preliminary Profile_ (Columbia, Missouri: Research Center of the School of Business and Public Administration, University of Missouri, 1967).

[47] George D. Young, "The Role of Political Parties in the Missouri House of Representatives" (unpublished Ph.D. dissertation, University of Missouri, 1958).

[48] Derge, _op. cit._

[49] Robert F. Karsch, _The Government of Missouri_ (11th ed.; Columbia, Missouri: Lucus Brothers Publishers, 1971), chapters 6, 7, 8, 9.

[50] Karsch, _The Standing Committees in the Missouri General Assembly_, _op. cit._

[51] A review of the 1970 census tracts, those completely within or where the major portion of the tract was within the area represented by blacks as defined by the legislative district boundaries, showed that the collective constituency in black-represented districts of the Missouri House was predominantly Negro (89.2%). U.S. Bureau of Census, Census of Housing: 1970, _Block Statistics_, Final Report HC (3)-135, Kansas City, Mo.-Kans. Urbanized Area (Washington, D.C.: U.S. Government Printing Office, 1971), pp. 24-46; U.S. Bureau of Census, Census of Housing: 1970, _Block Statistics_, Final Report HC (3)-137, St. Louis, Mo.-Ill. Urbanized Area (Washington, D.C.: U.S. Government Printing Office, 1971), pp. 97-146; _Election Laws of the State of Missouri_, 1969-70 (Jefferson City, Missouri: James C. Kirkpatrick, Secretary of State, n.d.), pp. 461, 476-478.

[52] _The Black Politician_ (Summer, 1970), p. 20, as cited by Walton, _Black Politics_, _op. cit._, p. 199.

[53] _Ibid._ The percentage of blacks in the Missouri House was 7.9. Those legislative chambers with higher percentages were the Ohio House (10.0), the Ohio Senate (9.0) and the Michigan House (9.0).

[54]See Clark, op. cit.; and Franklin, op. cit.

[55]Representative Leon Jordon was assassinated in July, 1970, before either the questionnaire was returned or the interview was conducted.

[56]Official Manual State of Missouri, 1969-70 (Jefferson City, Missouri: James C. Kirkpatrick, Secretary of State, 1970).

[57]State of Missouri, House Journal, 75th General Assembly, Volume 1, Regular session, compiled by James C. Kirkpatrick, Secretary of State.

[58]Kansas City Call, St. Louis American, and St. Louis Argus.

[59]Arthur F. Bentley, The Process of Government (Chicago: University of Chicago Press, 1908).

[60]Earl Latham, The Group Basis of Politics (Ithaca, N.Y.: Cornell University Press, 1952), p. 1.

[61]David B. Truman, The Governmental Process (New York: Alfred A. Knopf, Inc., 1951), p. 23.

[62]Ibid., pp. 23-24.

[63]Latham, op. cit., pp. 14-15.

[64]Ibid.

[65]Alan Fiellin, "The Functions of Informal Groups: A State Delegation," New Perspectives on the House of Representatives, eds., Robert L. Peabody and Nelson W. Polsby (Chicago: Rand McNally and Company, 1963), pp. 59-78, reprinted from "The Functions of Informal Groups in Legislative Institutions," Journal of Politics, XXIV (February, 1962), 72-91.

[66]Ibid., pp. 63-64.

[67]Ibid.

[68]Shibutani and Kwan, op. cit., p. 47.

[69]Truman, The Governmental Process, op. cit., p. 343.

[70]David Easton, The Political System (New York: Alfred A. Knopf, Inc., 1953), pp. 129 ff.; and A Framework for Political Analysis (Englewood Cliffs, N.J.: Prentice-Hall, Inc., 1965), pp. 50 ff. See also, Gabriel A. Almond and G. Bingham Powell, Jr., Comparative Politics (Boston: Little, Brown and Company, 1966), pp. 16-21.

[71]See Easton, A Framework for Political Analysis, op. cit., pp. 59-75.

[72]For a discussion on political socialization see Almond and Powell, op. cit., p. 24.

[73]For a discussion on political culture see Almond and Powell, op. cit., pp. 23-24, 50-72.

[74]For a discussion on political structures see Almond and Powell, op. cit., pp. 21-22, 42-49.

[75]For a discussion on the conversion function see Almond and Powell, op. cit., pp. 29, 98-127.

[76]For a discussion on system capability see Almond and Powell, op. cit., pp. 28-29, 190-212.

CHAPTER II

THE BLACK LEGISLATOR

     This chapter is devoted to a collective examination of the
black representatives. A general discussion of the nature of such
personal characteristics as class status, residency, age, education,
occupation, and sex will be offered.[1] In addition, the legislator's
commitments to his district and his association with ethnic organizations
or civil rights groups will be given attention. This discussion will
provide a basis for generalizing about the personal characteristics of
black legislators. Several studies which include general information
about the personal characteristics of the members of the Missouri
House will be drawn upon for purposes of comparison.[2] Although these
comparisons are not uniform, they will provide a foundation for noting
differences in characteristics of the black delegation from those
characteristics generally found for the larger membership. A comparison
of characteristics between black legislators and non-black House members,
during the period of 1969-70, will be offered where sufficient data
was available.

Class Status

     In state legislatures, much like the National Congress but to
a lesser degree, there is an over-representation of those persons coming
from middle-class and upper middle-class backgrounds. In the case
of the black legislators in the Missouri House the common background
could be defined as one of poverty and of the lower social-economic
class. There is, however, a major difficulty in comparing blacks to
the generally accepted and defined class system in the United States.
Blacks holding occupational positions of middle-class stature in terms
of the black community would probably be classified as low-class, at
least economically, by commonly accepted non-black standards. Generally,
the blacks referred to their family backgrounds as poverty stricken.
This was true even in cases where occupational categorization--such as
minister, barber, and farmer--would suggest a different categorization
by general standards.

     Elaine Burgess discussed the differences in class structure of
the white and black communities in her findings in Cresent City in 1960.[3]
Her categorization of the black class system would indicate that the
backgrounds of the Negro members of the Missouri House would place
them generally in the middle to lower class of the Negro community.
There were a few representatives whose backgrounds would require classification as lower class. Burgess defined the upper class as executives
of financial, insurance, and real estate firms; persons engaged in the

professions--doctors, corporation lawyers, college administrators and faculty members (professors); and owners and managers of large business and commercial establishments. The middle class included small business proprietors, lawyers in private practice, lower-rank college faculty (instructors), public school teachers, ministers, social workers, white-collar workers, service workers, skilled and semi-skilled workers. The lower class was composed of domestic workers and servants, unskilled labor, the unemployed and those whose income was derived from illegal activities.[4]

A common theme in the background of the legislators was that even though their origins were from families generally in the lower half of the class spectrum for Negroes, they generally expressed a feeling that they were brought up by the standards of middle-class morality. One legislator summed up the general expressions when he recalled:

> I came from a poor family with middle-class morality, a highly religious family. I think we had the middle-class ideas of working for the pay-off and appreciated cleanliness. . ./My/ family set a great deal of store on working around the house, supporting himself, and greatly scorning welfare programs or asking anyone to give you anything.

Recent decades, particularly since World War II, have brought blacks additional opportunities in education and employment, changing the nature of the Negro class system. Predominant among the changes is the social mobility which has occurred as a result of achievements in higher education. Whereas their families would be classified in the black class system at the lower levels of the spectrum, the black legislators themselves can be placed in categories ranging from the middle-class to the upper-class of the Negro community. For the most part, black representatives occupied upper middle-class positions in the Negro class system. A small proportion have reached positions which suggest an upper-class designation, but none falls below the middle-class category. The overall significance is that black assembly-men, much like their white contemporaries, over-represent the middle and upper middle classes of their constituencies.

Residency

Studies on state legislators also have shown that lawmakers generally have been raised in the area they represent or, at least, have resided there for the major portion of their lives. Generally, the black legislator in the Missouri House was born either in the state, or in the South and moved to Missouri in childhood. The place of birth for the legislators under study and the location of their public school education are shown in Table 2.1.

TABLE 2.1

PLACE OF BIRTH AND EDUCATION OF BLACK LEGISLATORS, MISSOURI HOUSE OF REPRESENTATIVES, 1969-70

Geographical Area	Birthplace	Public School Education
Missouri	6 (46%)	9 (69%)
Southern State	5 (38%)	2 (15%)
Mid-west (Illinois)	1 (8%)	1 (8%)
Northern State (New York)	1 (8%)	1 (8%)
	13 (100%)	13 (100%)

Earlier studies of the Missouri Legislature have shown that most representatives were born within the state. George Young's study showed that 147 of 185 representatives in the 1955 and 1957 sessions were born in the state.[5] Information on the House membership for 1969-70 shows that 124 of 142 (87%) non-black representatives were born in Missouri.[6] The data presented in this study show that blacks tend to have a higher rate of birth outside the state. This is partially explained by the rate of migration of blacks from the South to Northern cities witnessed in the past several decades. It is not particularly surprising to find that a major portion of the black representatives have migrated to a metropolitan area of the state from Southern portions of the country. It is interesting to note, as indicated in Table 2.1 that the majority of black assemblymen migrated rather early in life from the South, and that they received the bulk of their public school education in the state of Missouri.

The concept of lengthy tenure in one's district is applicable to blacks as well as other legislators.[7] Of the four blacks not educated in Missouri, one was from Illinois and claims to have lived in St. Louis, off and on, all of his life. Another has spent more than half of his life in St. Louis. Only two have not resided in the state for at least half of their lives. One of these two came to the state twenty years ago and the other eleven years ago. David Leuthold's profile of the Missouri Legislature during the 1965-66 session reported that 89 percent of the House members had resided in their districts for at least twenty years.[8] Consistent with this general pattern 92 percent of the black delegation had lived in their districts twenty years or more. With only one exception, the black

lawmakers in the Missouri House have lived in the general area of
their districts for the larger portion of their lives.

Age

Composite descriptions of lawmakers often include the characteristic of age. The median age of Missouri House members during the
1969-70 session was forty-five years.[9] Black representatives in
the House were insignificantly older, averaging forty-eight years.
This represents a decline in the average age, fifty-one years,
reported by Young in his study of the mid-fifties.[10] Whereas the
recent influx of the larger delegations of black representation has
been a partial result of the whole civil rights movement in the past
two decades in which young Negroes have performed vital roles,
there is no significant evidence to suggest that younger persons
are performing these legislative roles. A breakdown by age categories
for the black solons shows one member as sixty years or older,
seven members in their fifties, two members in their forties and
three representatives in their thirties.

In comparing the age distribution of black House members
with non-black House members some differences were found, as
illustrated by Table 2.2. Blacks were found to be slightly less
likely to be under forty years of age or above sixty than were non-
black members. The variations in these two categories are relatively
insignificant. More meaningful are those deviations in the middle-
age groupings. Whereas 60 percent of the non-black members were
less than fifty years old, a majority of the black solons had
become quinquagenarians. The age characteristics of the black
legislators in 1969-70 are similar to earlier studies of the Missouri
House. Hadwiger reported that a majority of the House membership
between 1947-56 had celebrated fifty or more birthdays.[11] On the
whole the age of Missouri state representatives has declined in
recent years. The black delegation appears to be an exception to
the trend toward younger representatives, at least for the 1969-70
session.

TABLE 2.2

AGE CATEGORIES, MISSOURI HOUSE OF REPRESENTATIVES[a],
1969 - 1970

Categories	Total House Membership	Non-black Membership	Black Membership
25-39	48 (30%)	45 (30%)	3 (23%)
40-49	47 (29%)	45 (30%)	2 (15%)
50-59	41 (25%)	34 (23%)	7 (54%)
60 and over	18 (11%)	17 (12%)	1 (8%)
No information	9 (5%)	9 (5%)	0 (0%)
Total	163 (100%)	150 (100%)	13 (100%)

[a]Note: Age is defined as the total number of chronological years attained by the individual legislator on the opening day of the 75th General Assembly, January 8, 1969.

Source: This information was tabulated from Official Manual State of Missouri, 1969-70 (Jefferson City, Missouri: James C. Kirkpatrick, Secretary of State, 1970), pp. 110-173.

Education

All of the members studied in this project reported they were high school graduates, and, with the exception of three representatives, all reported some higher educational training. Of these ten Negro members, five had graduated from college, three had received instruction at vocational or trade schools, and two others had had some college education. Of interest is the fact that none of the three black solons under the age of forty had received a college degree. One had attended college, however, and another reported that he was currently beginning to work toward a degree on a part-time basis.

The educational achievements of black assemblymen compare favorably with their House colleagues, as is shown in Table 2.3. Whereas a slightly higher percentage of blacks had training beyond high school, this is due primarily to a higher proportion of them having attended vocational and trade schools rather than to a higher proportion of their members attending college or graduate institutions.

The results of this research show a higher level of educational achievement than has been found in previous studies of the Missouri lower chamber. Studies by Young and Hadwiger showed only 60 percent receiving training beyond high school.[12] Leuthold's more recent study indicated a rise in training levels beyond high school. He found that 65 percent had experienced some form of higher education.[13] Whereas, the trend has been toward legislators with higher levels of educational achievements, the black delegation in the House has managed to avoid a deviating pattern of higher education with the training received at vocational schools.

TABLE 2.3

EDUCATIONAL ACHIEVEMENT, MISSOURI HOUSE OF
REPRESENTATIVES, 1969-70

Categories			
High school or less	44 (27%)	41 (27%)	3 (23%)
Some college or college graduation	48 (29%)	44 (29%)	4 (31%)
Graduate study	52 (32%)	49 (33%)	3 (23%)
Vocational or trade school	15 (9%)	12 (8%)	3 (23%)
No information	4 (3%)	4 (3%)	0 (0%)
Total	163 (100%)	150 (100%)	13 (100%)

Source: The information in this table was tabulated from Official Manual State of Missouri, 1969-70 (Jefferson City, Missouri: James C. Kirkpatrick, Secretary of State, 1970), pp. 110-172.

With reference to the education received by the black legislators, the racial composition of student bodies in their alma maters, as might be expected, was predominantly black. The only legislator who did not attend an all-black public school was educated in New York. Those legislators who attended vocational schools did so in black institutions. The black representatives who graduated from college, with one exception, received their degrees from Negro schools. Once again, the exception was the legislator educated in the East in a predominantly white institution. The only deviation from this pattern of training and education in black institutions was found for those representatives who attended graduate institutions.

A significant aspect of the above is that, for the most part, the black legislator, like his white colleagues, is considerably better educated than his constituents. This, of course, is typical of findings in previous inquiries into the personal characteristics of legislators. Additional significance can be attached to the fact that when attending an educational institution, the black legislator did so at schools designed for the black population. Only when black institutions were not available did the black legislator attend a predominantly non-black school. This is largely explained by educational segregation in Missouri until the past decade.

Occupation

The occupational composition of legislative bodies across the United States has shown a heavy predominance of members of the professions and business. Traditionally, and still largely true of today's decision-making bodies, these two general categories of occupations are highly over represented. Data on the Missouri House for 1969-70 supports this characteristic of legislators, as shown by Table 2.4.

Black representatives conform to established occupational patterns in one area, proprietorship, but deviate from the norm in the professional category. Seven members of the black delegation in the House were engaged in small business concerns--a security business, a tavern, real estate, insurance, banking, and a funeral home. Two black representatives were classified as professionals, one a lawyer and the other a journalist. Three blacks held jobs regarded as white collar--a production planner for a large industry, a salesman, and a union official. One member was employed as a deputy sheriff prior to his election to the House and was classified as a government employee.

A comparison of the 1969-70 occupational classifications in the Missouri House with earlier studies shows only minor differences. Hadwiger's study from 1947-56 reported professionals as 35 percent of the membership, business related occupations as 31 percent and farming as 17 percent.[14] Only two categories showed change of any significance: businessmen increased while farmers decreased. If any one factor can be isolated as the cause of this variation, it would be reapportionment.

TABLE 2.4

OCCUPATIONS OF MEMBERS OF MISSOURI HOUSE OF REPRESENTATIVES,
1969-70

Categories	Total House Membership	Non-Black House Membership	Black House Membership
Professional	52 (32%)	51 (34%)	2 (15%)
Proprietors	72 (44%)	65 (43%)	7 (54%)
White Collar	12 (7%)	9 (6%)	3 (23%)
Laborer	8 (5%)	8 (5%)	0 (0%)
Government Employee	2 (1%)	1 (1%)	1 (8%)
Farmer	8 (5%)	8 (5%)	0 (0%)
Retired	3 (2%)	3 (2%)	0 (0%)
Student	1 (1%)	1 (1%)	0 (0%)
Homemaker	4 (3%)	3 (2%)	0 (0%)
No information	1 (1%)	1 (1%)	0 (0%)
Total	163 (101%)	150 (100%)	13 (100%)

Source: This information was tabulated from Official Manual State of Missouri, 1969-70 (Jefferson City, Missouri: James C. Kirkpatrick, Secretary of State, 1970), pp. 110-173.

Although the black legislators conform to the changing pattern of occupational characteristics, there is some variation when comparing them with the non-black members of the 1969-70 session. The black delegation drew a higher proportion of its members from occupations classified as proprietors and white collar than did the non-blacks, and had a lower proportion in the professional category. There are several explanations for the lack of conformity by the Negro members of the legislature to the general pattern of occupational classifications. Most important has been the fact that it has been only in recent years that blacks had the opportunity to obtain the education needed for professional occupations. Where access to education was available, the average black was limited by the cost factor. Since talented blacks have had to turn to other occupations for opportunities black leadership clusters in different vocations. Black businessmen and white-collar workers occupy positions in their community which can be regarded as the upper levels on an occupational status spectrum. In essence, these two occupational categories simply fills the void of professionals in the black community. The general conclusion that can be made is that black representatives, like their colleagues, come from occupational backgrounds which are atypical of their constituents.

Sex

Like most other legislative delegations, the black group in the Missouri House is predominantly, though not exclusively, male. The proportion of male-female legislators is in accord with the general make-up of the total legislature. Since the beginning of the era of reapportionment and the one-man-one-vote rulings, the Negro delegation has had at least one woman member. The delegation for the 1969-70 session included one woman member, DeVerne Calloway.[15]

The legislator's commitments to his district

Most legislators have certain family or occupational ties in the constituency they represent, which would indicate a strong commitment or tie to the general area they represent. There were two factors related to the black community which provided the basis for a tentative hypothesis that blacks lacked this strong commitment to their constituency. First, the migration of blacks from rural areas of the Southern region of the country to the cities in Northern areas suggested a possible absence of strong family and community ties to a given geographical location. Secondly, it was thought that the limited nature of opportunities for supplying a person's financial livelihood would be such that the geographical boundaries of the district would be of little importance.

Contrary to expectations this inquiry produced convincing evidence that black legislators had strong commitments to their districts. Of the twelve legislators for which data was available, there is evidence that ten of these had family members residing in the areas they represented, i.e., married sons and daughters, sisters, brothers, parents and in-laws. Although most of the lawmakers had relatives outside the district as well, there did appear to be sufficient heritage lines inside the constituency to account for a general family commitment to the area.

Business or occupational commitments were not as strong as family ties. Assemblymen from Kansas City showed a strong commitment to their districts in terms of their occupations. Two owned or partially owned businesses in their districts. The sole black lawyer representative in the House maintained his office in his district. The fourth representative in the House did not maintain his office within the limits of his districts, but his occupation, real estate, is not a type which demands a central headquarters in the district for a commitment to exist. The focal point in this type of occupation is the location of real estate holdings. This legislator did have sufficient interest in his district to allow the researcher to conclude an occupational commitment to the district.

St. Louis Negro representatives did not show the same strong commitments. Of the nine legislators from the Mississippi port only four were actively engaged in operating their own businesses. Only one of these four conducted a business within the confines of his district. The other three operated businesses which had broader orientations than their constituencies. As a result, these representatives were required to be outside their districts a large portion of their time. Whereas some commitments did exist to the general black area, there is reason to suggest that for the most part these commitments did not stem from occupations.

Involvement in ethnic organizations

Are the blacks elected to the Missouri House the same persons who led and who are now leading the civil rights organizations? A unique facet of the backgrounds brought to the legislature by the black representatives is their involvement in ethnic organizations. In broader studies of legislators' backgrounds this would not be an area that would merit attention. As a result of the uniqueness of the racial heritage for the black person in this country, ethnic organizations are seen as a major component of this inquiry. The experiences of the past two decades bring this relationship between the black leader and the ethnic organization to a position of major importance.

Most black representatives have been or still are members of the National Association for the Advancement of Colored Persons (NAACP). In a national poll conducted by TIME magazine and Lou Harris, which was published in April of 1970, blacks, in general, gave this organization the highest rating in terms of respect.[16] It was not surprising that the NAACP should be found to be the black organization with which most black legislators affiliated, as shown in Table 2.5.

TABLE 2.5

BLACK LEGISLATORS' MEMBERSHIP IN ETHNIC ORGANIZATIONS

Organizations	Have held memberships	Current members	Have held leadership positions
NAACP	10	9	4
Urban League	3	3	1
CORE	4	3	1
Other	2	2	0
None	1	-	-

Source: The information in Table 2.5 was tabulated from interviews with black representatives.

Nearly all of the black lawmakers belong to or have held membership in at least one organization. One member, however, stated he had never belonged to any civil rights organization. The drop in memberships for the NAACP represents one legislator who reported that he was active as a younger person but drifted away from the organization. Two members of the House did not hold current memberships in any civil rights organization, and, be it noted, both of these were among the younger members of the black delegation. Their lack of memberships might be explained in a number of ways: (1) they might have grown disenchanted with the tactics and slow achievement pace of the organizations, or (2) they may have felt that no group was meeting the needs of their race, or (3) they plainly had no desire to belong to an ethnic organization. Although the data does not apply sufficient guidance for confident judgment, it is the impression of this writer that the lack of involvement by these two is explainable by indifference rather than by ideological reasons. The two appeared to be more interested in political gains and organizations than in the more comprehensive programs of civil rights organizations.

Whereas most black representatives did hold ethnic organization membership, only four of those serving in the legislature had played any leadership role for such an organization. This included one president of the Missouri Conference for NAACP chapters; one metropolitan NAACP president who also served as a board member for the Urban League; and an executive board member of the local NAACP chapter. The fourth is reported to have been one of the original founders of CORE, some twenty years ago, and has chaired several committees for the local NAACP in recent years. Representatives performing leadership roles in civil rights organizations amounted to only one third of the black House membership.

Another significant observation from this information is that the black lawmaker limited his civil rights activity to those organizations generally regarded as the conservative and middle-of-the-road groups. None of the legislators claimed to have belonged to any of the more militant or left-wing organizations, such as the Black Panthers, the Black Muslims or others. Like other persons in public office, the black legislator in the Missouri House holds memberships in organizations which would be classified as non-radical in nature.

Summary

This chapter has presented a description of the thirteen black legislators who served in the Missouri House during the 75th General Assembly. Beyond the initial identification of the individuals studied, the preceding pages presented a collective description of the personal characteristics of the Negro representatives. Where appropriate and available information existed, the personal characteristics of black assemblymen were compared with those of their non-black colleagues. For certain characteristics it was also possible to compare information from 1969-70 with data presented by earlier studies on the Missouri House. The result of the discussion has been the production of a basis for understanding the personal characteristics which the legislator brings with him to the legislative arena and how these characteristics may influence his performance as a legislator.

The information presented in the preceding pages paints a picture of the Negro legislator with many of the same personal characteristics as other state legislators. He has resided in the general area of his district for the major portion of his life. He comes from the same general age categories as his colleagues. He has attained a high school diploma and has received additional educational training. And he greatly over represents the masculine sex.

Deviations from findings of earlier studies are largely explained by the nature of his heritage. There is little basis for a comparison of social class, occupation, and certain aspects of education without controlling for the differences between the black and non-black communities in America. Deprivation of opportunities and denial of access to certain institutions have generally kept blacks from achieving the same standards and levels of status which are held by those who are non-black. It would be deceptive to judge the Negro achievements in certain areas against the general societal

standards which are usually the basis for descriptive analysis of
legislator characteristics. By setting the black legislator within
the environment of his own community, it is possible to conclude
that, relatively, he possesses the same general characteristics as
his non-black colleagues. Results of the presentation in this chapter
show this clearly in several areas. His family heritage and background represent a lower social-class status than is generally found
for state legislators, but his family back-ground generally represents
the middle ranges of the social-class system within the Negro community.
The black legislator's own social position would be in the middle
to lower middle classes in a broad categorization, but in terms of
his community he represents the upper middle class, and in a few
cases borders on the upper class. His occupation falls into the
small business or proprietor classification rather than the professional,
yet his occupation represents a position in the upper levels of the
Negro occupational scale. Finally, his educational achievements
at the college level are slightly lower than those of his colleagues,
but he has compensated for this deficiency by utilizing vocational
and trade schools to advance his training and in the process has
made himself atypical of the educational achievements of those in
the black community.

Two other rather unusual characteristics were also considered.
First, family and occupational ties to the general area of the
legislator's district were examined. Strong family commitments to
their districts were found among the black legislators. Strong
occupational ties, however, were not nearly as conclusive. Overall,
only a minority of the members indicated strong occupational
commitments to their constituencies. Secondly, the black legislator
was found to associate with groups which occupy the moderate-to-
conservative wing on a civil rights organization spectrum. Whereas
most of the legislators belonged to at least one such organization,
only one third of the House delegation performed any kind of leadership
roles for these groups. Little credence can be given to an assumption
that black politicians, especially legislators, are the same persons
who had led or who are now leading civil rights organizations.

Notes

[1]Data for this section came from information supplied by the
black legislators and from Official Manual State of Missouri, 1969-70
(Jefferson City, Missouri: James C. Kirkpatrick, Secretary of State,
1970).

[2]Don F. Hadwiger, "Representation in the Missouri General
Assembly," Missouri Law Review, XXIV (April, 1959), pp. 178-195; and
David A. Leuthold, The Missouri Legislature: A Preliminary Profile
(Columbia: Research Center of the School of Business and Public
Administration, University of Missouri, 1967); and George D. Young,
"The Role of Political Parties in the Missouri House of Representatives"
(unpublished Ph.D. dissertation, University of Missouri, 1958).

[3]Elaine Burgess, <u>Negro Leadership in a Southern City</u> (Chapel Hill: The University of North Carolina Press, 1960), p. 27.

[4]<u>Ibid</u>.

[5]Young, <u>op. cit.</u>, pp. 34-35.

[6]This information was tabulated from the <u>Official Manual State of Missouri</u>, 1969-70, op. cit., pp. 110-173. No information was available on eight of the non-black members.

[7]Districts as used to specify residency of legislators in this section are defined as the whole city in which they live. Because of the periodically changing nature of legislative district lines in the city and as a result of the gradual movement of the black population from one section of the city to another, residency among the constituents represented by the black legislator and the geographical limits of the district may not necessarily be the same.

[8]Leuthold, <u>op. cit.</u>, p. 4. There was insufficient information available in the <u>Official Manual State of Missouri, 1969-70</u>, to compare residency of non-blacks with patterns of the black legislators for the 75th General Assembly.

[9]Age is defined as the total number of chronological years attained by the individual legislator on the opening day of the 75th General Assembly, January 8, 1969. This information was obtained from <u>Official Manual State of Missouri, 1969-70</u>, <u>op. cit.</u>, pp. 110-173.

[10]Young, <u>op. cit.</u>, pp. 33-34.

[11]Hadwiger, <u>op. cit.</u>, p. 181.

[12]Young, <u>op. cit.</u>, p. 38; and Hadwiger, <u>op. cit.</u>, p. 183.

[13]Leuthold, <u>op. cit.</u>, p. 2.

[14]Hadwiger, <u>op. cit.</u>, p. 188.

[15]Following the death of Kansas City Representative Leon Jordon in July, 1970, his wife, Mrs. Orchid Jordon, was elected to fill the vacancy of the unexpired term. Thus, there were two black women in the House during the last few months of the 75th General Assembly.

[16]<u>TIME</u>, April 6, 1970, p. 28.

CHAPTER III

RECRUITMENT AND ELECTION OF THE

BLACK LEGISLATOR

Of all factors which might be suggested as influences on legislative behavior, none can be as vital as those which orient the individual to the political process and assure him of his seat in the legislature. Failure to work successfully through the political maze of recruitment and to emerge as the victor at the ballot box makes all other potential influences irrelevant. It is the comprehensive recruitment and election processes which produce the actors on the legislative stage, and it is to those processes that this chapter is devoted.

The recruitment process for this study included political orientations and experiences occurring before the individual considered seeking office, as well as factors which spurred the individuals to actively seek the role of a legislator. In this segment early orientations into the political system are discussed. Pre-legislative experience in political life is examined with attention to both public service and political party service. Factors which stimulated the individuals to accept the challenge of seeking a political office are considered. The styles by which the legislators were recruited are noted. Political party organization is discussed as it relates to the black legislator.

The second portion of the chapter focuses on the process in which legislators are chosen from among the several who aspire. Included is an examination of the competitiveness of the primary elections, a look at both the density and the intensity of the first electoral contest; consideration of legislative turn-over; and an analysis of the general election of black representatives.

The findings in the succeeding pages emerge from analyzing data, from several sources, pertinent to the described topic. Primarily, the information utilized in the first segment of the chapter was gathered in interviews with the Negro members of the Missouri House. The second portion of the chapter is based upon election data reported in the Official Manual State of Missouri, 1969-70.[1] In both cases the material is supplemented by reports found in the Negro-oriented newspapers in Kansas City and St. Louis.

Political Socialization and the
Recruitment Process

Interest in politics

In beginning it is necessary to ascertain the development
of personal interest in politics. One trend, appearing from the
discussions with the black legislators, was that their political
interest began rather early in life. As in the findings of the four-
state study by a group of scholars in the 1950's,[2] the black
legislators in the Missouri House developed their first interest
during or soon after the period of their formal education. Only three
of the legislators indicated that their interest had begun in relatively
recent years. Of these three, two are still young by standards of
political officeholding, as they are in their mid-thirties.

Three basic themes were presented as the source of early
orientations toward the active political arena. Like others who
become politically active, five black representatives received their
political baptism by working for particular candidates. Most of
those who received their initiation by this method did so rather
young. As one legislator recalled, "I have been in politics all of
my life. As a little boy I used to pass out the ballots for my
precinct." Another noted, "When I was eight years old, I passed out
pamphlets. . .and then I got interested in politics." This orientation,
however, was not necessarily one of youth. One legislator recalled
that his first interest in politics came as a result of working for
a neighbor during a primary election when he was in his early adulthood.

Secondly, five solons recalled that their political interest
was stimulated by the civil rights movement. This orientation may
be expressed as an awareness that the improvement of Negro conditions
had to come through the political system. One black reported that
early in his life he had been identified with militant groups of his
community. After a couple of years he began to doubt the success of
these groups in solving the problems of the black community. It was
then that he realized that, "The kind of government and the kind of
world that I wanted to build was through politics." He expanded by
saying, "I am convinced that the Negro will never get full equality
until he becomes fully cognizant and has a responsible role as a
political person." A colleague reported that he lived in a district
that was half black and half white and was represented by a white who
had definite ideas about black participation in his organization, which
was non-existent. As a taxpayer the black felt he did not have the
opportunity to discuss his problems with his representative. As a
result he developed an interest in political change.

A third theme, expressed by two assemblymen, related to
employment. First, employment led to political interest in that it
was through the political organization that jobs could be obtained.
One representative recalled, "I became interested in politics rather
young. In fact I was around nineteen years of age. The reason I was

interested in politics. . .was I didn't have a job." He reported seeking assistance from a political organization in obtaining a job and was able to get one, "even though it was just a part-time summer job." Secondly, the job one held demanded some political involvement. As a labor representative, the other legislator in this type was asked by his union to mobilize support in the black community for a particular congressman. Once he became involved in political action through his job, he developed an interest in politics which led to his own candidacy for office.

Whereas many persons obtained their orientation to politics by working in campaigns and as a result of employment or a lack of employment, the stimulus from the civil rights movement is unique. Although other minority groups in our society have used organized ethnic groups as a source of developing political interest, little can compare to the impact that the civil rights movement has had over the past decade and a half on Negro political participation and interest. Over the next few decades, the civil rights movement may well be credited in large measure with enlisting the interest of black youth in seeking public office.

Pre-legislative experience

As noted above, most black legislators in this study had developed an interest in politics long before they entered the legislative arena, and this interest was evident by the holding of public office or party office. The bulk of the membership of this group had some such experience prior to being elected to the legislature. For the most part, this experience was limited to performing roles within the political party organization.

It is clear, from Table 3.1, that nearly two-thirds of the legislators played a role within the party organization. Only one representative had held a public elective office prior to being elected to the legislature; he had served as an alderman in St. Louis. Another had held a city position as an appointed municipal judge. Pre-legislative experience was limited to only one position with two exceptions: the representative who held a local office also held a party position at the precinct level and another member reported having held an appointive position on the Federal Housing Authority as well as the party position of committeeman. Only four of the thirteen members had no experience in either a party or public position prior to their election to the Missouri House. Three of these, however, indicated that they had a rather long-time affiliation and membership in the local party organization. Nearly every member of the legislature from the black community had served some political apprenticeship before his or her election.

TABLE 3.1

PRE-LEGISLATIVE EXPERIENCE OF BLACK LEGISLATORS

Type of Experience	Number[a]
Party position at the ward level	4
Party position at the precinct level	4
Municipal elective office	1
Appointed to public position	2
None	4

[a]Two legislators had pre-legislative experience in more than one position.

Source: The information in Table 3.1 was tabulated from interviews with black legislators.

The findings here indicate that the path to a seat in the Missouri House for Negroes is greatly enhanced by being active in and serving in a party position at the grass-roots level. The results can further be said to show that the pre-legislative experience pattern for black state legislators does not deviate from the general trends found for larger groups of state representatives.[3]

Reasons for seeking office

Persons seeking public office accept the challenge for a variety of reasons, which are often complex and embedded in the individual personality. Many times the real reasons are hidden from even the closest observers. The expressed rhetoric of a candidate's decision to enter the thicket of elective politics, however, is generally valid as at least a partial explanation for his actions.

Two themes ran through the responses to the inquiry on why the black representatives sought election to the legislature. Most pre-eminent was that by serving in the General Assembly they could do something for other persons or for the community. This sentiment for humanity was expressed by seven of the twelve respondents. Typical of the responses were these:

I can't recall in my life when I haven't wanted to do
something for somebody. . .I wanted to be a legislator
because I would be in a position to do things. . .I enjoy
being able to increase this person's income, to raise
his standard of living. . .I think it is just the personal
satisfaction of being able to do things for people.

I felt that there were some changes that needed to be
/made/ and I felt I could contribute something to the
state as well as to my district.

The second most frequent response indicated a sense of
dissatisfaction with the persons and organizations in office at the
time they decided to seek office. Most of this dissatisfaction was
directed at white legislators who represented districts that were
largely black. Of the five who responded in this category, four did
so because they felt it was time to remove white representation from
their districts. There was one situation, however, where a black
representative indicated his sole reason for seeking office was
to remove a black legislator who was allegedly unconcerned with the
major problems of the black community. He cited the circumstance
of the 1967 disturbance in his community in which he and other black
officials performed a major peace-keeping function. The current
legislator recalled,

We had a state legislator who during the time of the
riots--we prefer to call it a civil disturbance--did not
show up at all. . .I decided that anybody that unconcerned
about problems as big as that ought not to represent
the district.

Style of recruitment

It is often difficult to distinguish between the reasons for
seeking office and the basic style of recruitment which is used to
encourage a potential candidate to place his name on the ballot. By
style of recruitment the concern is with the specific influences that
persuaded the legislator to file for office. The previous section
was intended to deal with the elements which made the candidate
accept the opportunity when it was proposed. In this section the
concern is with the forces that successfully persuaded the legislator
to seek public office.

A major factor for seven of the black legislators in their
original effort to win office was the support of some political
organization. Most of these can be defined as the regular Democratic
organization which controlled the district at the time of their
election. Of these seven, five responded that persons in the organization
requested that they consider the race. The other two indicated that
they had personally considered public service in the legislature,
but it was only after obtaining organization support that they made
the final determination to seek office. The remaining six, although

not supported by the party leaders in control of the party machinery at the time of their first election, were supported by independent Democratic organizations and groups within their districts. Most of the legislators in this group played leadership roles in the development of these independent organizations. Eventually the factions that gave support to the legislators succeeded in gaining control of the party machinery. Of the total group, during the 75th General Assembly only one representative did not belong to the dominant political party faction in his district. It is possible to conclude that the style of recruitment in black districts is heavily dependent upon the support of the party organization.

The political party organization

It is appropriate to follow the preceding comments with a brief look at the political party structure and its relation to the individual black legislators. In Missouri there has been no state-wide attempt to build a black faction within the Democratic Party. The past decade, however, has produced several strong black organizations at the grass-roots level of the political system. The real source of black influence on the party organization has been at the ward level in the two metropolitan areas of the state. The absence of centralized political leadership in the black community has produced a rather fragmented structure in the movement for political influence.

In St. Louis the black political organization is for all practical purposes fragmented by ward divisions. This does not mean that there is an absence of all cooperative efforts, for there do exist some limited efforts in pursuing the goals of the black political community. The point that needs clarity is that there is no unifying force which pulls the legislators together to form a comprehensive black organization.[4] Each committeeman generally controls the organization in his ward and in most cases plays an important role in determining the persons who become legislators in districts within his ward.[5] Although legislative districts cut across ward boundaries, the importance of the ward leader in the largest portion of the district is vital in terms of gaining support. The nine-member black delegation from St. Louis in the Missouri House is divided among loyalties to different black committeemen. During the 75th General Assembly three of the black committeemen themselves held seats in the legislature.

It is not absolutely impossible, however, to win election to the legislature outside the party organization in the black community in St. Louis. One freshman representative won election over the regular organization candidate. This independent organization proved successful in the legislative race, and it was reported that the legislator had his sights on taking over the ward organization.[8]

Black legislators from Kansas City present a picture which is somewhat different in terms of the party organization. In Kansas City a black organization emerged in the early 1960's and proved successful in uniting the black community within the Democratic Party organization. This faction labeled Freedom Incorporated captured control of the regular party machinery in all of the black wards except one. Three of the four black representatives from Kansas City sought office with the support and endorsement of Freedom Incorporated, including one of the major founders of the organization, Leon Jordon. The fourth representative from Kansas City had his own ward organization, The Brotherhood Democratic Club, but generally allied his group with the Regular Democrats, the old-line political faction in the city, rather than allying with the broader black faction.

The major point to be made about the party organization is that the legislators from Freedom Incorporated successfully unified a large portion of the black community behind the one political organization. While in St. Louis the black organizational structure is greatly fragmented among the various ward leaders, the black political forces in Kansas City have created an organization which encompasses all but one of the Negro wards.

Before leaving the brief discussion of party organizations in the black community, it is necessary to inquire into the willingness of black organizations to form alliances with organizations outside the Negro communities. In Kansas City, as mentioned previously, the Brotherhood Democratic Club generally allied with the "Regular Democrats" (as they were called by the blacks) faction for purposes of city and county elections. Freedom Incorporated, on the other hand, has served as a balancing force among the county's factions in the past several years. It formed alliances with different organizations while maintaining its independence in almost all city and county elections. Using its bargaining position as the balance of power between the old-line faction and the Committee for County Progress in Jackson County politics, Freedom Incorporated successfully elected two black county officials, and during the time of this study elected a black county chairman of the Democratic Party.

In St. Louis the political party structure is different. There has been little effort to form alliances or organizations on a base broader than the ward. This is partially due to the importance of the ward as a district for the election of city aldermen and the impact on state legislative politics by the ward organization dominant within the specific districts. As a result, the Democratic Party is fragmented along ward boundaries. Banfield and Wilson note the two general factors in St. Louis politics as the Mayor's Office Group and the County Office Group.[7] The Mayor's Office Group "stands for good government" and "civic progress," and has as its chief supporters "newspapers, downtown business interests and the middle-class wards."[8] On the other hand, the County Office Group consists of the St. Louis City County officeholders and members of the Board of Aldermen, and is mainly interested in obtaining jobs and favors. As Banfield and Wilson suggest, whereas there is sufficient patronage to tie this group together for control of the city, the ward committeemen bid against one another for support, and the result is a maintenance of independence for the ward committeemen.[9] The Negro ward leaders are among these committeemen. Although alliances are made outside the black community, these have been quasi-temporary in nature. The success of black candidates for office in city-wide elections has been severely limited. The black effort has been harmed by two factors. First, the Negro ward leaders have failed to agree on black candidates prior to elections, and some black leaders have given only nominal support to their black brothers.[10] Secondly, divided black political leadership and the maintenance of independent attitudes among ward leaders have resulted in stifling the formation of alliances with groups outside the black community which could contribute to the successes of black politicians.

While there is a difference in the style of politics between blacks in St. Louis and Kansas City, there is similarity in their political organizational behavior. The style of politics used by the blacks in both cities is in accordance with the prevailing style of the environment. The acceptance of dominant behavior patterns of political factions or groups in the community is witnessed by the approaches used by blacks in the two cities. Political influence in Kansas City is achieved by the building of more comprehensive organizations and alliances across ward boundaries, whereas the atmosphere in St. Louis is more inclined to encourage independence and fragmentation.

With regard to the black legislators themselves, however, the black organizations in St. Louis and Kansas City have maintained their complete independence, as there are no alliances which carry over into the legislative arena. The only exception to this general rule would be the Negro legislator from Kansas City who has tied his organization into a closer alliance with the "Regular Democrats" rather than the dominant black organization.

The Election Process

To gain entrance into the legislative halls, a Missouri legislator, like his counterparts in most other states, must win the support of the electorate on two occasions, the primary and general elections. In this section the black legislator is examined in terms of his success in meeting these obstacles and securing a seat in the state House of Representatives. First, let us consider the competitiveness in the black districts for these legislative seats.

Competitiveness in the primary election

Since all of the black legislators in this study are Democrats by party affiliation, they met their first electoral test for the 75th Missouri General Assembly in the Democratic Primary in August of 1968. In the primary elections the competitiveness in the black districts, as shown by Table 3.2 is greater than in other urban districts. A non-competitive district is defined as one where only one Democrat appeared on the ballot. A competitive district is where two or more persons sought the Democratic Party's nomination for the legislature. The information showing competitiveness in the primary is focused on the urban districts of the state, within St. Louis and Kansas City.[11]

TABLE 3.2

COMPETITIVENESS IN THE DEMOCRATIC PRIMARY, 1968

Type of District	Total number of districts	Competitive	Non-competitive
All urban districts	45 (100%)	33 (73%)	12 (27%)
Urban districts won by Republicans	7 (100%)	5 (71%)	2 (29%)
Urban districts won by non-black Democrats	25 (100%)	15 (60%)	10 (40%)
Urban districts won by black democrats	13 (100%)	13 (100%)	0 (0%)

Source: This information was tabulated from Official Manual State of Missouri, 1969-70 (Jefferson City, Missouri: James C. Kirkpatrick, Secretary of State, 1970), pp. 1340-48.

From the above table it may be concluded that there is more likelihood of competition in the Democratic Primary in districts where blacks win seats than in other urban districts. All districts that elected black legislators had a competitive Democratic Primary, whereas districts electing non-black Democrats were competitive only 60 percent of the time. There was greater competition in the Democratic Primaries in districts which eventually elected Republicans than in districts where non-black Democrats won the legislative seats.

What factors, if any, explain the higher competitiveness in the districts where blacks were elected to the legislature? There is one major factor which might explain the situation. In all of the districts defined as urban, all incumbents sought re-election with the exception of five. The five districts without incumbents were all districts which elected black legislators. The pattern found in this study supports the general conclusion that "primaries in which incumbents seek renomination are less likely to involve competition than are those in which no incumbent is running."[12] A second explanation, though there is no data in this study to give it support, is the competitiveness among black political leaders for political control. Since it has only been in recent years that blacks have been able to gain control of the political machinery in these legislative districts from organizations led by non-black politicians, different groups within the black community are competing among themselves for political control. The literature on primary elections has suggested that a strong party organization may discourage challengers to the incumbent or the party's choice for the nomination.[13]

The competitiveness factor can be clarified by examining the density of competition within legislative districts.[14] Density of competition simply refers to the number of candidates seeking the party's nomination in the primary. When grouping legislative districts the average number of competitors per district will be termed as the density score, as in Table 3.3 for the urban districts in 1968.

There were more candidates seeking the party's nomination in legislative districts where blacks won seats in the Missouri House of Representatives than in other urban districts, as shown in Table 3.3. When the districts were divided in terms of the presence of an incumbent, however, the districts electing blacks produced a different picture. Where incumbents were seeking re-election, the density scores for the districts electing blacks (2.25) and districts electing non-black Democrats (2.12) were nearly similar, with the black districts having only a slightly higher score. The major difference in the density scores was found in those districts electing blacks where the incumbent was not a candidate.

The difficulty of this analysis is that in districts won by non-black Democrats in 1968, all incumbents were candidates for re-election, which could be considered rather unusual. The overall significance of the density scores is that in 1968, in the urban districts where blacks won representation in the Missouri House, there was a higher level of density than in districts won by non-black Democrats. The dominant factor in the variation of density scores, however, appears to be the presence of an incumbent rather than one associated with the ethnicity of the district.

The number of persons seeking the party's nomination is only one indicator of the competitiveness of a legislative district. As important, if not more so, is the level of competition among those aspiring to be the nominee. This factor shall be referred to as the intensity of the election.[15] An intensity score for each legislative district was calculated by a formula devised to show the level of the competition between the nominee and his closest competitor. The score was reached by calculating the percentage of votes, of the total ballots cast, received by the winning candidate in the primary, and by doing the same for his nearest rival. When this was completed the score was determined by finding the difference between the two candidates; a higher score indicates a lessening of real competition between the candidates. The level of intensity in the Democratic Primaries in the urban districts is shown by Table 3.4. For the purpose of simplifying the information the scores are placed in one of four categories ranging from high to low levels in intensity. Also shown is the average of the individual scores for the designated groups.

TABLE 3.3

DENSITY OF COMPETITION IN THE DEMOCRATIC PRIMARY, 1968

Categories of Districts	Number of districts	Number of candidates									Density[a] Score
		0	1	2	3	4	5	6	7	8	
All urban districts	45	0	12	19	9	2	0	2	0	1	2.33
Urban districts won by Republicans	7	0	2	1	3	1	0	0	0	0	2.43
Urban districts won by non-black Democrats	25	0	10	10	3	0	0	1	0	1	2.12
Urban districts won by black Democrats	13	0	0	8	3	1	0	1	0	0	2.69
Urban districts won by black Democrats where incumbent was a candidate	8	0	0	6	2	0	0	0	0	0	2.25
Urban districts won by black Democrats where incumbent was not a candidate	5	0	0	2	1	1	0	1	0	0	3.40

[a]Density score expresses the average number of candidates per legislative district.

Source: This information was tabulated from Official Manual State of Missouri, 1969-70 (Jefferson City, Missouri: James C. Kirkpatrick, Secretary of State, 1970), pp. 1340-48.

TABLE 3.4

INTENSITY OF COMPETITION IN COMPETITIVE DISTRICTS,
DEMOCRATIC PRIMARY, 1968

| Categories of Districts | Intensity score[a] categories | | | | Average of District Scores |
	High 0-9.9	Medium High 10.0-24.9	Medium Low 25.0-49.9	Low 50.0-up	
All urban districts	6	7	11	9	34.8
Urban districts won by Republicans	1	2	2	0	18.5
Urban districts won by non-black Democrats	2	3	5	5	36.7
Urban districts won by black Democrats	3	2	4	4	39.0
Urban districts won by black Democrats where the incumbent was a candidate	1	1	2	4	45.1
Urban districts won by black Democrats where the incumbent was not a candidate	2	1	2	0	19.3

[a]Intensity scores are an expression of the closeness of the primary election by subtracting the percentage of votes received by the runner-up from the percentage received by the nominee. Example: candidate A received 55 percent of the votes and candidate B 45 percent. The intensity score for the district would be 10.0

Source: This information was tabulated from Official Manual State of Missouri, 1969-70 (Jefferson City, Missouri: James C. Kirkpatrick, Secretary of State, 1970), pp. 1340-48.

The inquiry into the intensity of competition produced several conclusions about competition in the legislative districts. First, in districts won by blacks there was generally a lower level of intensity in the primary election than was found in other urban districts. This needs some qualification, however, in order to produce an accurate picture.

Although black districts score slightly higher in general than other urban districts, there is a major difference in the scores when controlling for the presence of an incumbent in the Democratic Primary. In the black districts where the incumbents sought re-nomination the intensity scores were considerably higher than in the non-black districts where the incumbent sought re-election. Of course, as was noted earlier, all of the non-black incumbents did seek re-nomination. Where the black incumbent was a candidate the intensity of the primary election was quite low. Where the incumbent was absent in the primary the intensity score shows a higher level of real competition. This is generally the expected pattern of elections, and it is verified in this study by the similarity in scores for the Democratic Primary in districts where there was no Democrat incumbent, in the districts won by the Republicans, and in the five black districts where no incumbent was a candidate.[16]

Legislative turn-over and the black legislator

In examining the competitiveness within the legislative districts in the primary elections, the data have consistently shown the impact which the absence of an incumbent has on the elections. It has already been noted that there are only five urban districts in 1968 which did not have the incumbent as a candidate and these five were all districts won by blacks. The logical question to pose at this juncture is, what significance, if any, can be attributed to the five districts without incumbents?

Four black legislators who held seats in the House of Representatives during the 74th Missouri General Assembly did not seek re-election in 1968. In vacating their seats in the House, three sought election to higher political office. James Troupe filed as a candidate for Congress in the 1st Congressional District. This seat in Congress, due to redistricting, was for the first time (1968) one which the blacks could win. Troupe, having been one of the chief architects of the district in the state House, had ambitions of being Missouri's first black Congressman. Troupe, however, withdrew from the Congressional race on July 20, 1968, after William Clay, a black alderman, had received the endorsements of the vast majority of black organizations in the district.[17] Fearing the possibility that the blacks might divide their vote among the three black candidates (Ernest Calloway, husband of state representative DeVerne Calloway, was the other black candidate) and give the nomination to the lone white candidate, Troupe withdrew to give Clay additional strength.

The other two ambitious black incumbents sought seats in the Missouri Senate. They both ran against white Democrat incumbents in their bids for higher office. Raymond Howard, who vacated the seat in the 54th Legislative District, was successful in winning a Senate seat from St. Louis. Harold Holliday, from Kansas City's 10th Legislative District, fell short in his bid for the party's nomination in the primary.

Both gentlemen who sought higher office, and were defeated or withdrew, returned to the Missouri House. Both Troupe's ward organization in St. Louis and Freedom Incorporated in Kansas City were successful in having their candidates win the primaries where these incumbents were not candidates. In both cases the successful primary candidates withdrew so that Troupe and Holliday could return to the Lower House. Following the primary, Jackson Curry in the 53rd District in St. Louis withdrew, and Troupe was appointed by the Democratic City Central Committee to run as the replacement in the general election.[18] In Kansas City the 14th Legislative District nominee William Carson withdrew as "a strategy move which can be used by Freedom Incorporated to further strengthen the community's representation."[19] The ward committeemen and committeewomen of the district promptly renominated Holliday for the legislative seat. From the maneuvering that followed the primary in 1968, it seems rather obvious that the organizations in these districts had provided stand-in candidates for the black House members that had sought other political office.

The fourth black incumbent who did not seek re-election was John Conley of the 75th State Legislative District. Conley apparently was seeking to solidify his control over the 22nd Ward Organization in St. Louis, which he was successful in doing by winning election to the committeeman post in the 1968 primary. If Conley had a stand-in for his legislative seat, he was defeated. Leroy Malcolm, the successful candidate, had his affiliation with an independent Democratic organization.

The fifth legislative district without an incumbent was in an area where the black population had grown large enough to permit the success of a black candidate. The white incumbent in the district did not seek re-election. Whether it was for reasons other than fear of defeat by the blacks in the districts, is not known.

Previously it was noted that where incumbents were candidates in the black districts there was both less density and intensity with regard to the primary election as opposed to the districts where incumbents were not candidates. This, however, failed to deal with the question of the incumbent success in returning to the Missouri House. Of the eight districts where black incumbents were candidates, only six were re-nominated. This presents a rather high turn-over rate as compared to the other urban districts in 1968, where only two of the thirty-two incumbents were defeated. In both cases of black incumbent defeats, the organizations that prevailed

in the districts gave their support to the victorious challenger.
In the 71st Legislative District in St. Louis, the 26th Ward Democratic
Organization headed by William Clay gave its support to Nathaniel
Rivers over the incumbent Elsa Debra Hill. Rivers commented that he
preferred not to be a candidate for the legislature (he was an
alderman in St. Louis), but the organization felt that he would be a
candidate who could solidify the control of the organization over
challenges from Mrs. Hill and other forces in the district. Although
the rhetoric of the campaign appeared to have been rather heated, to
be expected with a split in the organization, Rivers defeated Mrs.
Hill easily by winning 68.9 percent of the vote.[20]

In Kansas City, Herman Johnson defeated incumbent James W.
Spencer in the 13th Legislative District. Johnson, who was concerned
with Spencer's lack of leadership for the black community in troubled
times, like the disturbance of 1967, sought and received the support
of Freedom Incorporated in his successful challenge. Johnson captured
45.2 percent of the vote as opposed to Spencer's 32.5 percent. A
third candidate received the remaining 22 percent of the vote.

Where black incumbents were defeated in the primary election,
density scores for the district were higher than for the races where
the incumbents were renominated. The scores were 2.00 and 3.00
respectively. It was also found, as might be expected, that in the
primaries where the incumbents were defeated, the intensity score
averaged 28.5, whereas in the districts re-nominating the incumbent
the scores averaged 50.6. Similar patterns were found in other urban
districts for 1968. When incumbents are defeated in primary elections
there were high density scores and lower intensity scores. These
patterns are not unique to districts where blacks are elected.

The general election

The preceding comments have been in regard to the first
electoral hurdle placed before those seeking to sit in the Missouri
House. Attention is now turned to the second hurdle, the general
election. All black legislators in the Missouri House came from
dominant one-party areas, St. Louis and Jackson County.[21] As noted
in previous tables, only seven of the forty-five House seats from these
areas were won by Republicans in 1968. The remaining thirty-eight,
which includes the thirteen black seats, were dominated by the
Democrats. The level of general election competition in these
Democratic controlled districts is shown in Table 3.5. For comparative
purposes the districts won by blacks are shown separately.

TABLE 3.5

GENERAL ELECTION RESULTS IN URBAN LEGISLATIVE DISTRICTS
WON BY DEMOCRATS, 1968

| Category | Unopposed | % of vote for Democrats | | | | | Average % of vote received by Democrats |
		50.0-59.9%	60.0-69.9%	70.0-79.9%	80.0-89.9%	90.0-100.0%	
Non-blacks	1	5	10	6	3	0	68.7%
Blacks	2	0	1	0	4	6	88.2%

Source: This information was tabulated from Official Manual State
of Missouri, 1969-70 (Jefferson City, Missouri: James C. Kirkpatrick,
Secretary of State, 1970), pp. 1340-48.

Much of the general election opposition put forth by the Republicans
in these urban districts was minor at best. As the author of an earlier
study on the Missouri House stated,

In many instances the general election opposition to the
winning candidate was only token, especially in Kansas City
and St. Louis, where the Republican Party filled its tickets
regardless of their chances.[22]

The results of this study certainly substantiate those findings, especially
in the districts which elected blacks.

Two aspects of the general election call for further comment with
regard to the districts where blacks emerged victorious: the existence
of actual competition and the intensity of that competition. Only three
urban Democrats were elected in 1968 without Republican opposition, and
two of these were black.

The existence of real competition in the districts, however,
cannot be determined by the mere presence of a name under the Republican
label. The actual strength of the other party can only be determined by
reviewing the election results. The strength of the Democratic candidates, as shown by Table 3.5, indicates the weakness of his Republican
opposition. The table shows that the urban districts won by Democrats
can easily be defined as Democratic dominated districts. But one factor
standing out in the table is that the districts where blacks were elected
were more strongly Democratic than were the other urban districts. Only
one of the eleven black Democratic candidates with opposition received
less than 70 percent of the vote, whereas fifteen of the twenty-four non-

black Democrats received less than 70 percent of the vote. Further, the only Democratic candidates with Republican opposition who managed to receive 90 percent or better of the votes cast were six blacks. The average percent received by the Democratic candidates with Republican opponents summarizes the strength of Democrats in the black districts: black Democrats averaged 88.2 percent of the votes while non-blacks averaged twenty percentage points less, 68.7 percent.

Summary

The presentation in this chapter had as its objective the understanding of the influences and factors which affect the selection of legislators from the black community in Missouri. Vital to this discussion have been those components which impelled the individual to pierce the boundary between ordinary citizen and political activist. The initial concern was with the elements that gave the future legislator his introduction into the political system. The sequence of events and influences, which propelled the legislator from the initial entry into politics to a role of policy-maker, provides information vital to understanding the behavior of the black assemblyman.

The dominant facet of both the recruitment and election processes for the black legislator has been the political party organization. The role which the political party played in the overall selection of the legislator began early in the political development of the individual and continued as the major influence through the successful struggle at the ballot box. Most legislators cited the political party organization as the chief source for their personal interest and involvement in the political system. The legislator's initial orientation to politics came through campaign work for other political candidates and, in limited cases, by assistance from the political organization in locating employment. Pre-legislative experience in political roles was largely the result of holding a position within the political party organization at the ward or precinct level. Nearly two-thirds of the legislators had performed one of these roles prior to his election as a legislator. The majority of the black representatives entered their first race for the legislature with the support of the political organization which controlled the party hierarchy in their districts. During the session studied, all but one of the assemblymen sought office with the blessing of the dominant political organization in their districts.

The party's importance in the election contest is shown by the low level of intensity in actual competition, as exhibited by the election returns in the primary and general elections. Whereas all black districts had competitive primary elections, those districts with incumbents showed a lower level of intensity than did other urban districts in 1968. In the general election the strength of the Democratic Party in districts where blacks won seats in the legislature was considerably stronger than in other urban districts. Not only was there a lower level of Republican opposition, but the average percentage of votes polled by the black Democrats (88.2%) was nearly twenty points higher than that of his white colleague in the party. A major indicator of the party's influence on the selection process was found in the examination of the turn-over rate of House members. The political party organization in two of the thirteen districts managed to replace incumbent legislators with persons more to their liking. This was a higher rate of incumbent defeat at the polls than found for other urban districts in 1968. In two cases incumbent legislators who sought higher political office, and were defeated, regained their seats in the legislature when the party organizations in their districts had conveniently provided stand-in candidates for the primary election.

In the recruitment process it is difficult to separate the influences of the political organization, when it is a Negro organization, and the civil rights movement. Inasmuch as the development of the Negro involvement in politics and the selection of public officeholders has been one of the products of the overall civil rights movement in the past several decades, there are suggestions that the civil rights program has had an influence on the Negro legislator. A large portion of the Negro legislators made some notation of race among the reasons why they wanted to become a representative. Several entered the legislative contest because of dissatisfaction with certain white legislators. They also cited their desire to do something for those in the black community. In discussing the development of their original interest in the political system, one of the themes which ran through the legislator's remarks was the awareness of the importance of politics in achieving the desired goals for the black community.

Notes
_____

[1]*Official Manual State of Missouri, 1969-70* (Jefferson City, Missouri: James C. Kirkpatrick, Secretary of State, 1970), pp. 1296-1307, 1340-1348.

[2]John C. Wahlke, *et al.*, *The Legislative System* (New York: John Wiley and Sons, Inc., 1962), chapter 4.

[3]John C. Wahlke, *et al.*, *op. cit.*, pp. 95-101.

[4]For a discussion on the party organizational structure see Edward C. Banfield, *Big City Politics* (New York: Random House, 1965), pp. 123-127, and Kenneth E. Gray, *A Report on Politics in St. Louis* (Cambridge, Mass.: Joint Center for Urban Studies, 1959, mimeo).

[5]Edward C. Banfield and James Q. Wilson, *City Politics* (New York: Random House, 1963), p. 136.

[6]A short discussion on this point and Representative Malcolm is found in the column "Big City Shop Talk," *St. Louis Argus*, Feb. 14, 1969, p. 13.

[7]Banfield and Wilson, op. cit., p. 124.

[8]Ibid.

[9]Ibid.

[10]Al Wallace, "Big City Shop Talk," St. Louis Argus, August 23, 1968, p. 13.

[11]State legislative districts defined as urban are districts 1-16 and 18 in Jackson County and districts 50-77 in St. Louis City.

[12]V. O. Key, Jr., American State Politics: An Introduction (New York: Alfred A. Knopf, 1956), p. 175.

[13]Frank J. Sorauf, Party Politics in America (Boston: Little, Brown and Company, 1968), p. 217.

[14]Ibid., p. 216.

[15]Intensity corresponds to qualitative standards of competition discussed by Sorauf, Ibid., p. 216. See also, Leon D. Epstein, Politics in Wisconsin (Madison: The University of Wisconsin Press, 1958), pp. 134-135; and Frank J. Sorauf, Party and Representation: Legislative Politics in Pennsylvania (New York: Atherton Press, 1963), pp. 114-115.

[16]Key, op. cit., pp. 172-178; and Sorauf, Party Politics in America, op. cit., pp. 216-218.

[17]St. Louis American, July 25, 1968, p. 1.

[18]St. Louis Post-Dispatch, November 3, 1968, p. 21.

[19]Kansas City Call, September 27, 1968, pp. 1, 4.

[20]An example of the nature of the campaign is a suit filed by Mrs. Hill against Clay and Rivers charging that they "caused false and libelous matters to be printed, composed and circulated for the purpose of injuring and damaging her." The report contended that Clay and Rivers "did willfully publish material stating that Representative Hill had been convicted of being a prostitute." St. Louis American, August 1, 1968, pp. 1, 17.

[21]For a discussion on party competitiveness and classification in Missouri see Robert F. Karsch, The Government of Missouri (11th ed.; Columbus, Missouri: Lucas Brothers Publishers, 1971), chapter 3.

[22]Young, op. cit., p. 28.

CHAPTER IV

ATTITUDES AND PERCEPTIONS OF THE

BLACK LEGISLATOR

Knowledge of basic attitudes and perceptions held by public officeholders can provide a basis for understanding some patterns of behavior among these officials. It is not important here to determine the sources of attitudes (or socialization) but rather to describe briefly the views of black legislators on selected relevant topics. Essentially the focus will be on the result of socialization that has taken place in the individual and how it is translated into a group attitude by the composite of those who form the group under study.

The attitudes and perceptions uncovered in this study can be placed into four separate categories. Perceptions and attitudes which were felt to have a major impact on the Negro lawmakers were those concerned with race relations, the concerns of the black urban community, the political system, and the relationship between constituents and the legislators. Attitudes on race relations were expressed when the legislator defined the concept of "Black Power," identified the methods of protest he viewed as legitimate, and commented on the topic of integration. The legislator's views on the concerns of the black community were expressed during a discussion with the author on community goals and the problems of education, welfare, housing, and employment. His perceptions on the role of blacks in the political system formed the basis for understanding the political attitudes of the black legislator. Finally, the type of representational role claimed by the Negro legislator, together with his perceptions on the communication process between himself and his constituents, was examined.

The data utilized for the conclusions were gathered primarily from interviews held with the Negro legislators. In a few cases the information gathered in the interviews was supplemented by responses to questionnaires. Additional insight into attitudes and perceptions was obtained by researching the Negro press in Missouri during the general period of the study.

Attitudes on Race

Racial attitudes have created considerable controversy within American society in the past two decades. The volatile nature of this issue is still evident in many segments of society. When ethnic minority groups, such as the one studied here, begin to achieve success by placing members of their group in the decision-making structures of society in a quantity large enough to be a significant factor, attitudes concerning race become salient. The rhetorical tone and methods which minority representatives choose to express their attitudes on race questions will certainly be a factor in the legislative process. Militant, demanding rhetoric may produce a reaction wherein proposals by the minority group representatives are given little credence or assistance by the dominant group members. On the other hand, a moderate attitude or expression can relieve areas of potential tension and result in a productive working relationship with the non-minority group members. Persons representing racial minority groups, however, do have a responsibility to their constituencies to call attention to their group's problems and to promote the alteration of the deteriorated conditions which confront those of minority status. The ability of the minority group representative to walk the tight-rope of race relations, without alienating the dominant racial group in the legislature while acquiring desired changes for those of his own heritage, marks his success as a political figure.

Attitudes possessed by the Negro House members in Missouri are important in describing their performance as legislators. Following is a brief examination of racial attitudes as expressed by the black assemblymen. Although this probe into racial attitudes is shallow and touches only upon a small area of the potential, it provides an overall view of attitudes held by black legislators. Three general areas of racial attitudes form the substantive basis for this discussion: the definition of "Black Power," the forms of racial protest accepted as legitimate, and views on integration.

"Black Power" in recent years has developed as the major slogan of the black movement. Disagreement over the meaning of this slogan has created a schism not only between certain segments of the white and black communities, but also within the Negro community itself. As Joel Aberbach and Jack Walker said in their discussion of "Black Power:"

> A slogan like "Black Power" has no sharply defined meaning,
> it may excite many different emotions and may motivate
> individuals to express their loyalty or take action for
> almost contradictory reasons.[1]

In this study the concern is with how the black legislator in Missouri defined the slogan "Black Power." Ten of the black members of the Missouri House defined the term, and with differences. Four of them defined "Black Power" as meaning the exercise of influence in the political system: the process of utilizing the black vote in an effort to overcome problems faced by black persons. One legislator stated it simply as "Voting Power." One representative who viewed "Black Power" as meaning political influence suggested that its true meaning lay in obtaining better qualified blacks as well as more representation.

A second interpretation of "Black Power," given by three members, equated it with "Green Power." One legislator remarked there

is "no power in 'Black Power' but a lot of power in 'Economic Power'."
The economic development of the black community was felt to be the focus
of "Black Power." The obtaining of greater economic resources would
strengthen the black community to a position where blacks could influence
society. Those expressing this view of "Black Power" felt that real
political power was dependent upon the development of economic power in
the black society.

Finally, there were three members who viewed the concept, in a
broader sense, as a slogan for societal involvement. One legislator
gave his definition of "Black Power" as a "eulogy of black people to
compel action which is favorable to black interest." It serves as a
rallying point for the black community to achieve a part of the action,
whether it be political, economic, or social. When a given issue is at
stake, the concept provides the basis or the ideology for obtaining the
desired results. This is generally the meaning given the term by the
largest portion of blacks. Aberbach and Walker reported in their survey
of blacks that the term was most often defined "as a call for equal
treatment and a fair share for Negroes, or as an appeal for racial
solidarity in the struggle against discrimination."[2]

The black members of the Missouri House generally gave a meaning
to "Black Power" which represents the concern for bringing the black
community into a position of equality in the total society. Even though
the individual definitions varied in their focus, the general implication
was an ideology which the blacks can use in achieving a fair share in the
total community. This is not different from the overall meaning given
the concept of "Black Power" by persons such as Stokely Carmichael and
Charles Hamilton:

It is a call for black people in this country to unite, to
recognize their heritage, to build a sense of community.
It is a call for black people to begin to define their own
goals, to lead their own organizations and to support those
organizations.[3]

Little variance can be found when contrasting the definitions
used by the black legislators and those of a more activist background
such as Carmichael. The negative meaning frequently given to the concept
of "Black Power" has come from the use of this slogan by black militants
in efforts to rally groups for purposes of protesting black conditions.
Often the rhetoric suggests forms of violence as possible solutions.
Aberbach and Walker, however, reported that generally "blacks certainly
do not interpret the term the way whites do, they do not see it as
meaning racism, a general take-over or violence."[4]

What methods do the black representatives view as appropriate
for implementing this ideology into positive action? This question
naturally follows and most certainly needs some attention if the race
attitudes of the black assemblymen are to be gauged properly. The black
legislators were nearly unanimous in their response to a question asking
whether or not they felt "riots or other types of violence were appropriate

54

methods for protesting conditions of the black community." All but one of the eleven who responded disagreed with such protest tactics. One legislator, who did not personally condone violence as a means of protest, commented that such action has produced favorable change in the situation of the American Negro. In responding to a second question on methods of protest, the seven respondents, with one exception, viewed civil disobedience tactics to be generally successful in bringing attention to Negro needs. The lone dissenter felt that the council table approach was the most successful means of producing change in black communities.

In essence, the black legislators in the Missouri House felt a need for some ideology which can serve as a focal point for improving the conditions of the black community. They recognized a need for some force to bring awareness to the black problems and to provide a basis for unifying the black community. They believe the concept of "Black Power" can do this, but it must be used in its non-violent form to be accepted by those seated in the state House of Representatives. Two separate situations where individual legislators expressed, in action, their attitudes toward race disturbances and violence can be used to illustrate the basic attitude found among the black legislators.

In the spring of 1968 racial disturbances occurred in Kansas City. The leadership of Freedom Incorporated, the powerful black political faction in that city, played a prominent role in keeping the disturbance from becoming a major riot. Included in that leadership were three blacks who served as legislators during this study. An editorial in the Kansas City Star reported the role of these political figures.

> At the time of the April disturbances in Kansas City, Freedom Incorporated leaders were among those working hardest to cool the situation, maintain order and save lives and property. Many of them did so at considerable personal and political risk.[5]

Students at Lincoln University, the traditionally Negro university in Missouri, were involved in a disturbance in the spring of 1969. Apparently student grievances stimulated the situation. The St. Louis Argus reported the role played by black representative "Jet" Banks in quieting the disturbance.

> Much of the credit for preventing a possible disastrous situation from occurring if the students and police authorities had a confrontation is given to state representative "Jet" Banks. Banks requested fifteen minutes with students before Attorney General Danforth served the court's restraining order on the students. After Banks discussed the ramifications of the situation if the order was violated, students voted to give up the building /Student Union/.[6]

Attention is now turned to a vital area of race relations that could affect black politics in general, and certainly black legislators. This is the question of residential segregation. Although there are now laws which prohibit discrimination on a racial basis in housing, the fact remains that blacks are still living in neighborhoods that are predominantly black. Since it is these black areas that are electing the black legislators in the state of Missouri, questions were asked the representatives as to their attitudes on residential segregation.

Generally, the Negro legislator felt that residential integration was desirable. Only two of the ten representatives responding to this inquiry viewed residential integration as undesirable. In response to a question about residential integration and the impact this would have on the success of black politicians, the legislators generally expressed a feeling that it was not necessary to rely on areas that were predominantly black for the election of Negroes. Only two of the nine Negro legislators responding to this question viewed the predominantly black areas as having a major impact on the success of blacks in politics. Although the legislators responded positively toward residential integration, there remains some question as to what role blacks could play politically in totally integrated neighborhoods. It would seem that a high degree of integration would dilute the possibility of black persons serving in the state legislature. Also, the legislators in this study came generally from economic situations which would permit their movement away from the poverty stricken inner-city, but with only one possible exception they all resided in black neighborhoods.[7] Although the black legislators view residential integration as desirable and as having no impact on black representation, there remain certain factors which suggest that this is idealistic rhetoric and that by their actions they see an advantage in retaining the ethnic neighborhood. This is not to suggest that the black legislator will perform his legislative duties in such a manner as to make it more difficult for blacks to integrate. On the contrary, he works hard for fair and equal opportunities legislation in housing and in other areas of discrimination, but by choice he will probably retain his identification with the black neighborhood and community.

Black Community Concerns

Racial equality and the conditions of the city's ghetto have been the subjects of considerable attention in the past decade. It is to be expected that black leaders would beat the drums of despair and prejudice which have been the battle cry of the Negro movement in recent years. The black political leaders who served as the focus of this study willingly discussed the concerns and the problems in the black community. Their perceptions of the objectives for the Negro community and the perplexing difficulties which confronted those of their race differed little from those expressed by the non-political leadership of the black movement. They expressed their goals for the black community in terms of achieving equality among races and, more directly, of achieving desired improvements in the social-economic status of their race. The concerns of the black community as expressed by the Negro representatives are noted by the general categories in Table 4.1.

TABLE 4.1

BLACK COMMUNITY CONCERNS

Categories	Number of black legislators identifying issue area[a]
Civil rights	12
Economic (job opportunities and employment, black business)	8
Education and job training	6
Welfare	6
Housing	4
Other (crime, community organizations, and family stability)	3

[a]The black legislators referred to more than one substantive area when discussing community concerns.

Source: The above information was tabulated from interviews with the black legislators.

In one form or another, all twelve black legislators interviewed for this study expressed a desire for the achievement of equal status for blacks. As one legislator remarked, "My personal goal has always been. . .that black people. . .have the fullest opportunity. . . available under our system of government." The desire for equal status brings forth an implied, although not necessarily the same, supposition that race loses its meaning when societal interaction takes place. One representative suggested that we live in a society which "should ignore race, creed, or color." Several legislators, however, spoke in terms of needing to develop organizations and positive psychological attitudes in the black community in order to achieve the desired status. The need for black awareness, followed by the organization of blacks who are motivated and concerned, must be met prior to the achievement of an equal position in society. Generally, the attitudes expressed were directed at the full development of the black community. Legislation adopted by deliberative bodies such as the Missouri General Assembly provides only a part of the total development. All the legislature can do is guarantee legal equality and provide opportunities for development through various programs. The remainder rests with the community leadership in their communication with the persons at the grass-roots level. The legislators accepted the limitations upon their official roles, but generally agreed that they had a role to play in the overall development. Their primary concern was with the use of the state political system to provide the opportunities for development.

A second concern expressed by the black representatives was related to economic development. According to them, lack of money serves as the root of most problems found in the black community. Several legislators spoke of the need for black enterprise or business. One legislator related the cause of black family instability as being directly related to inadequate financial resources in the black community. The chief concern expressed was the lack of capital to develop black business, which they perceive as employing black persons and as a result would hopefully provide more and better jobs with increased family income.[8]

Most legislators agreed, however, that training is necessary to achieve this long-term economic development. Education and job training are needed, not only in the public schools and colleges, but also in occupational employment areas of skilled and semi-skilled labor. As a group the Negro legislators felt the state should play a role in the development of these areas. Better educational facilities in the ghettos, improved higher educational opportunities for the college-qualified student, and job-training programs for those now unemployable were all areas which needed state attention, according to the Negro solons.

Representatives from the black community were quite concerned with the general state of the welfare program and saw job training and education as a means of getting persons off the welfare rolls. One legislator reported, "Blacks now are not reliant on welfare as they have been in the past; they are trying to get out and help themselves." A St. Louis representative said, "I have been able to show them /Welfare recipients/ that they can't feed their families on welfare. . . they can't educate their families on welfare. . .you can't accomplish anything on welfare." He went on to describe how his political organization is attempting to give some basic training to those on welfare rolls so they can locate jobs. The hard part he found was going out and finding the persons and "convincing them that this /welfare/ is not the thing to do." Most agree that by offering training and employment the number of welfare recipients would decrease. They did not feel, however, that welfare programs should be curtailed. Their common concern was making welfare programs more meaningful. Several suggested that the state should make adequate payment allotments so that training could be accomplished.

It was also argued that certain procedures and regulations be altered in the current welfare programs. For instance, the current waiting period for investigation did not provide for meeting immediate needs of destitute persons. Having to wait until the welfare investigation can review an applicant's situation did not provide a solution to immediate needs. As one Negro legislator said, "If I come to you and say I need bread now and you tell me you have to wait until next month, I have got to investigate you, then you are not helping me too much." A veteran legislator told of his six-year struggle to change the requirements of the Aid-to-Dependent-Children Program, to permit fathers to be present in the home while allowing the mother to continue receiving assistance.

Two general conclusions were drawn from the discussion on welfare programs. The Negro representatives were concerned with changing some basic mechanics of the present programs to make them more beneficial and realistic to the needs of the recipient. On the other hand, the lawmakers seemed to be committed to structuring new programs which would take people, particularly blacks, off the welfare rolls on a permanent basis.

Housing was the final problem expressed as a concern in the black community. Two themes were present in the discussion on housing. One was the desire for the integration of residential areas. The other was the need for the replacement of deteriorated and inadequate housing in the ghetto areas.

This short discussion on the social-economic problems or concerns in the black community results in the conclusion that the problems in the inner-city perpetuate one another. When the legislators identified the concerns of their community, they generally talked of several of the areas noted in the preceding paragraphs. The conclusion is simply that the problems are often inter-related. One cannot get a job because of lack of training, and thus is destined to the welfare rolls, which results in the inability to afford adequate housing units and often serves as the cause of crime and family breakdown. Because of the circulatory nature of the problems in the black community, it appears that assistance must be sought in several areas of concern.

Political Attitudes

Political leadership for blacks in American society has gained great momentum in the past decade. The number of blacks holding positions at both municipal and state levels has increased tremendously. In the Missouri legislature alone, the number of black representatives has more than tripled since 1960, going from four to thirteen. Several questions were posed to the subjects of this study to gauge their views on the future of blacks in politics, their political aspirations and expectations, and the political process as an effective tool for meeting the problems of the black community. Their responses provided some indicators of black attitudes and expectations for the political system in which they perform.

Responding to a question on the future of blacks in politics, the representatives unanimously agreed that the prospect for black politicians is definitely positive for the approaching years. In a second question the assemblymen were asked if they felt blacks could

be elected from areas that are not predominantly Negro. Their response
to this inquiry was mixed, half of them indicating a future in these
areas, and the other half hesitant in actually foreseeing a time
when blacks could be elected in areas basically populated by non-blacks.
Those who anticipated a future for black politicians beyond the Negro
community did so with some expectation that this would come as a
result of bargaining and as a balance-of-support approach.

Basically there is total agreement that in predominantly
Negro-populated political divisions black politics will thrive. The
1968 elections in Kansas City and St. Louis legislative districts,
both House and Senate, showed the black leaders applying considerable
pressure on the white incumbents who represented portions of the black
community. Districts where blacks make up the majority of the
population are now electing black legislators. Some of the political
expectations are already being realized in larger political areas, such
as St. Louis City and Jackson County. In St. Louis the 1970 elections
produced the first black city officeholder. One legislator, who is also
a ward organization leader, remarked, "We are in the process of launching
a program of another black in a city-wide position." A second ward
leader-legislator from St. Louis observed, "We are close to having a
black mayor. . .I think within at least four to eight years." Jackson
County obtained two black county officeholders in 1968, and in 1970
the county Democratic Party Committee selected the head of Freedom
Incorporated as the chairman of the county committee. One Kansas
City representative expressed expectation that there would be a black
mayor and a black Congressman from his city.

One third of the legislators foresaw a future for blacks in
winning a state-wide office. "We are thinking the time will come when
we can be elected on the basis of merit and what people believe in. . .
without regard to. . .color," is the way one representative viewed the
future. Another legislator commented:

In view of the loyalty and support that black people have
given the Democratic Party, we feel we are entitled to
positions on the state level. Now black people are
becoming more sophisticated as far as their voting is concerned.
They've been voting for white persons ever since they
began to vote, and today unless there is a black person on
the ballot, they are not too particular about voting. And
this is the attitude we are going to have to take unless
/they/ support some black person state wide.

The implications of this statement are simply that the forces in the
Democratic Party must become aware of the contributions the blacks are
making to them politically and respond with similar opportunities for
blacks, or else the black organization will begin to change their role
in the election process.

In order for a black to win a state-wide campaign, however,
the blacks suggested two criteria need to be met. Most obvious is that

"it is going to have to be a particular individual, one who can appeal
to both black and white." There is little doubt that only an extraordinary
black man could be successful at this level. Satisfaction of this
criteria alone does not make the election of a black person probable.
It is the second condition which suggests some feasibility for future
expectations. Simply, it is the ability of the black organization to
unite and bargain with other political forces. One legislator responded
by suggesting that the hope for state-wide office lay with the development of a struggle between differing groups and factions of the party.
As a result, through the balancing support, the blacks could gain the
opportunity to elect a black officeholder.[9] Regardless of what approach
is used by the black organization, there are--in the eyes of some black
representatives--rays of hope for state-wide success.

After establishing the belief among black legislators that
there is a political future for Negro politicians, it is interesting to
examine their own aspirations and expectations for higher political
office. Only one of the twelve legislators interviewed definitely
expressed a lack of political ambition. The remaining legislators,
either by their political action or rhetoric, indicated aspirations for
other political offices. The lone unambitious legislator might be
explained partially by the fact that she was the only woman member of the
black delegation in the Missouri House. Whereas she claimed to have no
personal desire for higher office, she could be intimately linked to
political aspirations: her husband was a candidate for Congress in 1968.

The remaining representatives gave various responses to the
inquiry on aspirations. Six said that they would not object to serving
in the State Senate before their retirement from politics. One
representative, who was elected to the Senate in 1970, indicated that
he would be interested in a state-wide office. One legislator reported
his ambition was to return to the municipal legislative body in his
city. Another revealed his ambition when he became a Congressional
candidate in 1968. The other three gave no indication of a specific
office, but responded in such a manner as to indicate that higher
office was in their political thinking. Since most black solons
expressed a desire for higher public office, logic suggests a second
inquiry into their ambitions: Do black legislators expect to achieve
their political goals? A distinction must be made between aspirations
(goals, desires) and achievement expectations (the belief that the goal
will be accomplished).[10] This point is especially pertinent for black
politicians since there are only a limited number of blacks who have
been politically successful in electoral jurisdictions which are not
predominantly Negro.

Black assemblymen indicated that their achievement expectations
depended upon the drawing of political boundaries. This was particularly
true of those desiring seats in the higher body of the Missouri General
Assembly. Expectations hinged on the manner in which Senatorial Districts
would be drawn in the 1971 redistricting. All of those with sights on
the Senate hinged their expectations of success upon the composition of
the new districts. Most of the respondents were hopeful that the new
districts would favor their own interests. But, as Banfield and Wilson

observed, there is often conflict among individual groups as to what would constitute the most advantageous approach to districting.[11] Each legislator hopefully awaited the drawing of districts which would enhance his personal aims.

As a result of their involvement one would expect to find the subjects of this study holding positive attitudes towards the political system. On the other hand, there could be some justification for the development of negative attitudes. The failure of the system to meet the demands and needs of the black community or, if not a complete lack of success, the inevitable slowness of a legislative system in handling demands, could produce a feeling bordering on alienation. This might be particularly characteristic of members of a racial minority who have experienced rejection from society, as have the Negroes in earlier periods of time. The principals in this pursuit were asked if they felt the political system could produce the results which they desired for the black community. Their responses were accompanied by mild criticism toward the system but, in general, they all agreed that the goals they held for the community must be achieved through the orderly mechanisms of law and policy making. Comments from the legislators ranged from the need of new personalities in the system to such remarks as "it takes time sometimes" and "we have got to work awfully hard at it." In balancing the values of systematic change with the deficiencies in the current political structure, the black legislators expressed a belief in the current system as the best method for producing desired changes. The representatives do not reflect any of the rhetoric that is often linked with the militants of the black movement. Although it would be erroneous to call these legislators conservatives, in general they reflect a perference for the status quo with regard to the nature of our political system.

Constituency Relations as Perceived by the Black Legislators

In discussing the black representative and the orientations which influence his decision-making in the legislature, it is necessary to give some attention to his perceptions of constituency relations. In this segment the concern is with the representative's views toward his role as a representative and the communication process between the legislator and his constituents.

In defining their roles as representatives the black legislators were in agreement that their own constituents were their first responsibilities. They all concurred, however, in a feeling of responsibility for the total black community in the state. Thus, the Negro assemblymen performed a representative function, not only for their constituencies, but also for an ethnic group in the state. Although an analytical distinction between these functions is possible in describing the legislator's perceptions on representation, it is difficult pragmatically to justify such a distinction. Since the constituencies electing black House members were predominantly Negro, little difference can be seen in the performance of legislative representation for the legislator's constituencies and for the black population residing in districts electing non-black assemblymen. The legislators themselves noted the lack of distinction between the needs of blacks in their own districts and other blacks in the state. One legislator advanced this point of view when he stated, "I would certainly think that we have a responsibility to try to solve the racial problems throughout the whole state." Although the black legislators viewed their responsibilities to their constituency and to the total black community in the state as their first interests, they did express an attitude that in situations where their constituency and black interests were not predominant, they felt compelled to perform their legislative roles in accordance with the best interest of the whole state.

For the legislator to gauge constituency expectations there must be some form of communication between the representative and his constituents. Communication can take several forms. In response to a question related to legislator-constituent contact, four general types of communication were reported by the black representatives. These methods of communication differ considerably in form and style.

Commonly a legislator has a large amount of constituent contact through his mail. For the black legislator, however, mail played only a minor role in the communicative process with his constituents. The Negro representatives in the Missouri House reported that their mail was relatively light. Major portions of the mail they did receive from their district was generated by some organized group. Educational organizations were mentioned as those groups most vocal--the P.T.A., the Catholic schools, and school personnel. Several legislators commented that their mail came generally from places other than their districts. One black assemblyman reported, "Most of my correspondence comes from outside my district," and a colleague remarked, "I do not receive a volume of mail from my constituents. I get mail from everybody else in the world." Several black legislators explained the lack of the mail volume by expressing a belief that blacks are "not fully cognizant. . . that communicating with a legislator or any politician has a pay-off." Another expressed the belief that "black people are different. . .they won't take the time to sit down and write you a letter."

A second method of constituent-legislator contact can be labeled formal contact. Formal contact, as used here, refers to those structured activities where the representative appears before constituent groups (giving speeches or serving on discussion panels). Generally, this is a device for disseminating information from the legislator to the constituent. However, most would agree that this type of contact is many times vital in the flow of information from the opposite direction, from the constituent to the legislator. Simply, as a result of the formal appearance the legislator is able to receive feedback through questions and comments. As for the black House members, this process of communication played only a limited role. Most admitted to having only limited exposure to their constituents in formal contact.

A third form of communication is informal contact, the day-to-day association with constituents in unstructured contacts. These activities included on-the-street contact, association through mutual memberships held in various organizations, and contacts through business. The black legislators described this as the basic form of communication which they had with their constituents. One representative talked of maintaining direct relations with his constituents by serving on boards of different organizations in his district. The legislator contended that because his constituents were aware of his identification with various organizations there was little "compulsion among /his/ constituents to communicate with /him/." Another legislator, who claimed to know one fourth of his constituents by name, discussed contact with his constituents by saying, "They call me, meet me on the street. I see them at social gatherings--anywhere-- friend-to-friend talking." Others suggested that their organization headquarters provided a place where they could see constituents daily and discuss problems. Every black political organization had some type of headquarters which provided a general meeting place for groups and persons in the district. Finally, those who had businesses reported that these offered them opportunities for informal contact with constituents.

One final area of communication between the legislator and his constituents, which can be classified as legislator-initiated, is the one-way flow of information from the legislator to his constituents. This includes those processes by which the representative attempts to inform his constituency as to his actions and reasoning, as well as the issues before the legislature of concern to his constituents. Examples are columns written by legislators for publication in the local press, and newsletters periodically mailed out to constituents. All of the black legislators indicated that they had made attempts to communicate with their constituents by the use of one of these methods.

A considerable amount of legislator-constituent communication centered on the performance of the broker function by the representative. All of the legislators acknowledged that they spent a major portion of their public service time aiding some constituent or group of constituents in their dealings with the state bureaucracy. This type of contact focused generally on one of three areas: assisting a person who was on some form of state assistance program (welfare), helping a constituent find employment, or obtaining a state license to engage in some type of business, or aiding with a tax problem. The legislators noted that many of these requests were related to some area of public business that was not directly related to their job as a state legislator. For instance, many of the requests for assistance were in dealing with city administrations.

Summary

Legislative behavior may be partially elucidated when the legislator's personal orientations affecting the performance of lawmaking functions are known. The preceding discussion in this chapter has described several orientations with the hope of providing a clearer understanding of the attitudes and perceptions held by black legislators. In the discussion were the statements of the Negro lawmakers on general topics of race, politics, black community concerns,

and relations with their constituencies. The orientations expressed
provide a foundation for the understanding of black behavior patterns
within the legislature.

Like all kinds of leaders, the holder of a formal office
must rely upon others for the necessary support to maintain his position.
For the black legislator, like other political officeholders, the
holding of political power is predicated upon the maintenance of
support within the Negro community.[12] In order to preserve their
positions the legislators must be aware of the concerns of their
constituency. Lack of such an awareness could result in the withdrawal
of support at subsequent elections. The need for communication
between the legislator and his constituents must be met. The Missouri
Negro legislator described informal contact as the basic form of
this communication. Unstructured day-to-day conversation with persons
in their districts was all-important. The black assemblymen saw
formal organized contact and mail communication as performing only
limited roles in the process of relating to their constituencies.
Although all of the representatives claimed to have initiated some form
of one-way communication by the use of newsletters or newspaper
columns, this method was considered to be of minor importance in
reaching the voters. In his relations with the citizenry the black
legislator saw the broker function as his primary purpose.

The Negro legislator in Missouri, as elsewhere, must define
the role he will assume in performing his duties as a representative
of his constituency in the legislative arena.[13] From the information
gathered by this researcher, the black solon perceived his role as
primarily one of responsibility to the black community he represented.
He also viewed himself, however, as a representative agent for all
members of his minority group in the state.

The conflict between integration and segregation is important
for the politics of an ethnic minority. This is especially true for
those of Negro heritage. Although the black legislators in this
study claimed to support residential integration, they were also
cognizant of the fact that the composition of political districts
was important to the political future of blacks.

Where black legislators had political aspirations, the
expectation of goal achievement depended upon electoral jurisdictions
in which the Negro population would be the dominant group. The
political future for electing blacks by a voting populace where
Negros did not constitute a dominant group was seen as possible, but
only probably if two conditions were present: (1) a unique black
personality, and (2) a political atmosphere that would make it
possible for a cohesive black political organization to enter into a
coalition with other political groups.

Influencing the orientations of the black legislators in
the Missouri House are the goals which they hold for the black
community. Recent authors have defined goals of Negro political

leadership in terms of status or welfare goals.[14] Status goals "are those which seek integration of the Negro into all phases of community on the basis of equality."[15] Welfare goals "are those which look to the tangible improvement of the community or some individuals in it through the provision of better services, living conditions or positions." [16] Although all of the legislators in this study expressed a desire for the achievement of racial equality (status goals), they saw their primary officeholder role as directed toward welfare-oriented goals. The concerns of the black community were defined as the needs to improve social-economic conditions of economic development, education, job training, welfare programs, and housing.

In defining the current concept of "Black Power," the legislators viewed the term with reference to economic and political power, and as a slogan for black involvement. Regardless of the precise definition stated, the term was used as a slogan to overcome problems now existing in the black community.

In achieving the goals defined for the black community, the legislators held orientations which represented a moderate as opposed to a militant view.[17] The House members of the Negro ethnic group in Missouri viewed non-violence protests as legitimate means of demonstrating the conditions of the black community. Furthermore, the lawmakers agreed that improvements in the black community can best be achieved through maintenance and support of the governmental system.

Notes

[1]Joel Aberbach and Jack Walker, "The Meaning of Black Power: A Comparison of White and Black Interpretations of a Political Slogan," American Political Science Review, LXIV (June, 1970), p. 367.

[2]Ibid., p. 387.

[3]Stokely Carmichael and Charles V. Hamilton, Black Power: The Politics of Liberation in America (New York: Vintage Books, 1967), p. 44.

[4]Aberbach and Walker, op. cit., p. 373.

[5]Kansas City Star, June 21, 1968, p. 12.

[6]St. Louis Argus, May 16, 1969, pp. 1, 14a.

[7]During the period of this study Missouri's Attorney General John Danforth filed an ouster suit against Negro Representative J.B. "Jet" Banks on the grounds that Banks did not reside in the legislative district which he represented. The Supreme Court of Missouri disallowed Danforth's suit, ruling that no justifiable question was presented in the case. State v. Banks, 454 S.W. 2d 498 (1970).

[8]A discussion on black business which suggests that this
view is the result of an historical myth among the prominent members
of the black community can be found throughout E. Franklin Frazier's
Black Bourgeoisie: The Rise of a New Middle Class (New York: The
Free Press, 1957). Particular emphasis is given this point in Chapter
VII, pp. 153-173.

[9]For an excellent discussion on various strategies employed
by black political organizations see Harry Holloway, "Negro Political
Strategy: Coalition or Independent Power Politics." Social Science
Quarterly, LXIX (December, 1968), 534-47.

[10]A discussion on this point can be found in Herbert H.
Hyman, "The Value Systems of Different Classes," Class, Status and
Power, ed. Reinhard Bendix and Seymor Martin Lipset (2nd ed.; New
York: The Free Press, 1966), pp. 488-99.

[11]Edward C. Banfield and James Q. Wilson, City Politics (New
York: Random House, 1963), p. 88.

[12]Everett Carll Ladd, Jr., Negro Political Leadership in the
South (New York: Cornell University Press, 1966), pp. 44-45.

[13]For a discussion on representational orientations see John
C. Wahlke, et al., The Legislative System (New York: John Wiley and
Sons, Inc., 1962), chapter 12.

[14]James Q. Wilson, Negro Politics: The Search for Leadership
(New York: The Free Press, 1960), chapter 8; Donald R. Matthews and
James W. Prothro, Negroes and the New Southern Politics (New York:
Harcourt, Brace and World, Inc., 1966), pp. 191-195; Ladd, op. cit.,
chapter 4.

[15]Wilson, op. cit., p. 185.

[16]Ibid.

[17]Discussions on the various styles of Negro political leadership
can be found in Wilson, op. cit., chapter 8; Ladd, op. cit., chapter
4; and Matthews and Prothro, op. cit., pp. 186-191.

CHAPTER V

THE BLACK LEGISLATOR AND THE ORGANIZATIONAL

STRUCTURE OF THE HOUSE

A legislative body has a need for some systematic framework
which can direct and coordinate the group's activities. The performance
of these tasks can be referred to as leadership roles. One of the
common functions performed by a group's leadership is distributing
the group's work or tasks among the membership. In a legislative body
this commonly requires that a system of committees be established
for the management of the group's policy-making function. These two
phenomena--leadership and the division of labor--provide the basis
for the discussion in this chapter. In both cases the role of the
black solon is the primary concern.

Leadership and the Black Legislator

Leadership in a legislative body can be described as being of
two basic types, chamber and political party. There are two kinds
of chamber leaders: one performs a presiding function for the legislative
chamber and the other performs a leadership function for the committee
system. The Speaker and Speaker pro tempore perform the former
function, while the latter role is fulfilled by committee chairmen
and vice-chairmen. One distinction between the chamber leader and
the party leader is that one performs a task for the total body
while the other performs a task for a legislative sub-group, the
political party. A second distinction is based on the eligibility
of the individual member to serve in a leadership role. In most state
legislatures only certain members have access to chamber positions,
those who identify with the dominant party,[1] whereas all members--
assuming that all members identify with a political party--can seek a
party position, regardless of the majority-minority status of their
political party in the legislature. Leadership positions in the
political party are commonly referred to as the floor leader, whip,
and caucus officers. The tasks they perform are primarily party
oriented rather than chamber oriented. The difficulty in distinguishing
between these two types rests in the fact that the political parties
in most partisan state legislatures serve as the basis for chamber
leader selection.[2] As is commonly the situation, those who serve as
chamber leaders, especially those performing the presiding function,
are also, at least informally, political party leaders. Furthermore,
the majority floor leader, although primarily a political party leader,
also in many legislatures serves as the effective manager of the
chamber's deliberations.

Political party affiliation

Party affiliation is important in Missouri, as it is for most other state legislative bodies, since the majority political party fills the chamber leadership positions with its own members. During the 75th Missouri General Assembly the Democratic Party was the majority party in the House of Representatives.

Affiliation with the Democratic Party has dominated the partisan alignment of black Americans since the 1930's.[3] Since the incipience of this study, there has been no expectation of any deviation from this practice when identifying the political party adopted by the black representatives. All thirteen of the black House members identified with the Democratic Party.[4]

Positions of chamber leadership

Since the black assemblymen were members of the dominant political party in the Missouri House, they were potential candidates for chamber leadership positions during the 1969-70 session. This is true since they were members of the legislative sub-group, the Democratic Party, that selected the individuals who filled the presiding leadership roles, and the group from which the committee leadership positions were filled. Neither of the presiding offices was occupied by a Negro during the period studied. Some leadership positions in the committee system, however, were filled by blacks. The blacks benefited from the majority position of their political party affiliation when two of their members received appointments as committee chairmen and seven as vice-chairmen.

Positions of political party leadership

Positions of political party leadership, like the chamber positions performing presiding functions, excluded blacks in the 1969-70 session of the Missouri House. On the surface this may suggest that blacks have been passed over in the selection processes for party leadership. This can be misleading, however, since during the previous session of the Missouri General Assembly a black representative, James Troupe, served as the Democratic Party's caucus chairman. According to Troupe, he did not wish to succeed himself in that position for the 1969-70 session.[5] A newspaper report, however, suggested that racial considerations were responsible for his not retaining the position in the 1969-70 session. The article reported:

> State Representative James P. Troupe, Jr.,. . .was ousted
> as House Democratic caucus chairman at the House re-organization
> meeting last Monday in Jefferson City. Representative
> Troupe planned and maneuvered the redistricting bill through
> the House which finally resulted in the City of St. Louis
> having a Negro Congressman in the 1st Congressional District.
> Although Troupe did an excellent job, there are those who
> dislike the idea of a Negro having the power that Troupe
> had and exercised during the past session of the legislature.[6]

An examination of leadership positions in the Missouri House with reference to blacks suggests two basic trends. First, black House members performed only limited roles. Second, the leadership positions they did hold were not of major authority or responsibility, nor were they positions which they would have held if the Republican Party had been the majority party.

The Committee System and the
Black Legislator

Legislative committees have been described as "microcosms of the assembly" or "little legislatures."[7] They occupy a position of major importance in the lawmaking process. The traditional assessment of their role can be appreciated by recalling the words of Woodrow Wilson in 1885: "The House sits, not for serious discussion, but to sanction the conclusion of its committees. . .it legislates in its committee rooms."[8] Wilson's view of the role performed by committees in the National Congress is still true today, both for state legislative bodies and for the national legislature. It is the committees that handle the bulk of legislative decision-making in all American legislative bodies.

The function of committees in the Missouri House is the same as in other legislative structures. As Robert Karsch states:

The increasing variety and technical complexity of modern laws make it impossible for the whole chamber to undertake the preliminary processing of even the major bills. Without the spade work accomplished in committee--investigation, study, recommendation-- the legislature could not get its work done.[9]

In the Missouri House the selection of committee chairmen and the assignment to committees are entirely "the prerogative of the Speaker."[10] He permits the individual legislators to submit their committee preferences to him, but he is under no obligation to follow the preferences. Not only is he free to make committee assignments as he wishes, but he also has the power to assign bills to the individual committees, as is true in most other states.

Legislative leaders frequently make it a practice to assign most of the important bills to a few committees.

Those are committees dominated by members loyal to the legislative leadership. The result is that some committees are burdened with bills and others remain inoperative; some members are overworked and others have little to do when the committee sessions are held.[11]

Black committee assignments

During the 75th General Assembly the Negro members of the House were represented on half of the committees appointed by the Speaker. Of the forty committees appointed by the Speaker, the thirteen black members occupied seats on twenty-one. The committees to which black members were assigned are shown in Table 5.1. The Negro House member averaged 2.77 assignments, which was a lower average of assignments per member than for other groups that session, as shown by Table 5.2.

TABLE 5.1

COMMITTEE ASSIGNMENTS OF BLACK REPRESENTATIVES

Committee	Total number of members	Number of Democratic members	Number of Black members
Accounts	7	4	1
Appropriations	31	23	1
Atomic Energy and Industrial Development	13	8	3
Bills Perfected and Passed	2	2	1
Commerce	8	5	2
Education	32	23	1
Elections	15	10	1
Employment Security	5	3	2
Federal-State Relations	10	6	3
Fees and Salaries	12	8	1
Government Organization	10	7	1
Insurance	18	12	2
Judiciary	13	9	1
Labor	25	17	4
License	8	5	2
Local Government	11	7	1
Military and Veteran Affairs	7	5	2
Miscellaneous Resolutions	7	5	1
Motor Vehicle	8	5	2
Municipal Corporations	25	18	3
Public Health and Safety	13	8	1

Source: _Official Manual State of Missouri, 1969-70_ (Jefferson City, Missouri: James C. Kirkpatrick, Secretary of State, 1970), pp. 186-189.

TABLE 5.2

NUMBER OF COMMITTEE ASSIGNMENTS BY PARTY AND RACE

Category	Number of members	Number of committee assignments	Average number of committee assignments
All House members	162[a]	478	2.95
All Democrats	108[a]	319	2.95
Black Democrats	13	36	2.77
White Democrats	95[a]	283	2.98
Republicans	54	159	2.94

[a]Does not include the Speaker, who did not serve on any committees.

Source: _Official Manual State of Missouri, 1969-70_ (Jefferson City, Missouri: James C. Kirkpatrick, Secretary of State, 1970), pp. 188-189.

Ranking of Committees by work load

In order to provide a clearer understanding of the committee assignments held by the black House members, it is helpful to use some mechanism to show the degree of work performed by the individual committees. In this study the referral of bills to committees is used to measure committee work load. Although the number of bills handled by a committee is not necessarily an accurate measure of the work performed, some bills require more attention than others, it nevertheless does represent a tangible indication of the work load.[12] Karsch, in using the same measure, argued, "In fact, the committees that have the general reputation of being the influential committees do regularly receive the larger number of referrals."[13]

The number of bill referrals to the forty standing committees in the House during the regular session of the 75th General Assembly is shown in Table 5.3. The rating of each committee was devised by a formula based upon the number of bill referrals to each committee and what would have been an "ideal" equal division of labor among the functioning committees. Functioning committees were defined as those which received at least one bill referral. Some 1,299 bills were referred to committees in the House during the session. These

included 1,045 House Bills, 190 Senate Bills, 57 House Joint
Resolutions, and 7 Senate Joint Resolutions. Thirty-five of the
forty standing committees in the House functioned with regard to
reviewing and acting upon legislative bill referrals. Committees
which did not handle a single legislative referral were the committees
of Accounts, Legislative Research, Rules, State Fiscal Affairs, and
Bills Perfected and Passed. An ideal division of labor for the
thirty-five functioning committees would have been the assignment
of thirty-seven pieces of legislation to each committee. The ranking
of the committees was based upon this ideal referral rate.
Committees classified as A committees, those which had the largest
work load, were selected on the basis of having at least twice the
number of referrals (74) as the ideal referral rate. The B
committees were defined as those which handled at least one and one-
half times the ideal referral rate, but less than twice the ideal
referral rate (56-73). Those committees which receive referrals at
a rate of one-half (19) to one and one-half (55) the ideal referral
rate were classified as C committees. Committees receiving less
than one-half the ideal referral rate, but at least one bill, were
classified as D committees. Those non-functioning standing committees
with regard to referrals were given an E classification. The only
exception to this classification of committees on the basis of the
ideal referral rate was the Appropriations Committee. The nature of
this committee's work merited its placement in the top category,
although it handled only twenty pieces of legislation during the
1969-70 session.[14] Overall, seven committees were rated A, four
B, ten C, fourteen D, and five E.

TABLE 5.3

BILL REFERRALS TO STANDING COMMITTEES

Committee	Number of Bill Referrals[a]	Committee Ranking[b]
Judiciary	139	A
Economics	97	A
Government Organizations	94	A
Education	90	A
Local Government	82	A
Fees and Salaries	80	A
Appropriations[c]	20	A
Constitutional Amendments	65	B
Civil and Criminal Procedure	65	B
Social Security and Retirement	61	B
Ways and Means	60	B
Motor Vehicle	44	C
Elections	43	C
Municipal Corporations	42	C
Public Health	36	C
Insurance	30	C
State Institutions	30	C
License	29	C
Roads	27	C
Banks	26	C
Commerce	25	C
Workmen's Compensation	18	D

TABLE 5.3 (Continued)

Committee	Number of Bill Referrals[b]	Committee Ranking[b]
Agriculture	18	D
State Parks	17	D
Labor	16	D
Internal Affairs	16	D
Mines and Mining	9	D
Atomic Energy and Industrial Development	5	D
Inter-State Relations	4	D
Federal-State Relations	3	D
Military and Veteran Affairs	2	D
Miscellaneous Resolutions	2	D
Dairy and Livestock	2	D
Employment Security	1	D
Flood Control	1	D
Accounts	0	E
Bills Perfected and Passed	0	E
Legislative Research	0	E
Rules	0	E
State Fiscal Affairs	0	E

[a]Includes House Bills, Senate Bills, House Joint Resolutions, and Senate Joint Resolutions.

[b]The committee ranking is based upon the relation of the actual number of bill referrals to a committee and the ideal referral rate. The ideal referral rate is the number of bills which would have been assigned to each functioning committee (those which had at least one bill referral) if bills were referred equally among the committees. Ideal referral rate was 37 (1,299÷35). The committees were then ranked in relation to the ideal referral rate (IRR) as follows:

75

A at least, 2 x IRR (37) = 74 referrals
B 1½ x IRR, but less than 2 x IRR = 56-73 referrals
C ½ x IRR, but less than 1½ x IRR = 19-55 referrals
D less than ½ x IRR, but at least 1 bill referral = 1-18 referrals
E no bill referrals

[c]Although the Appropriations Committee does not receive a large number of bill referrals, it was given an A ranking because of the important nature of the legislation it considers.

Source: State of Missouri, House Journal, 75th General Assembly, Volume 1, Regular session, compiled by James C. Kirkpatrick, Secretary of State, pp. 2260-2349.

Committee work loads and committee assignments

By taking the committee rankings as a criterion of the importance of the role the committees play in the House, it is possible to evaluate the type of committee assignments which were given the black representatives. The committee assignments of the Negro House members with regard to the work-load ranking of the committees is shown in Table 5.4. The black delegation had representation on six of the seven committees in Category A, but did not hold one seat on any of the B committees. Thus, they lacked having any member on five of the eleven most active committees.

The committee leadership appointments held by black House members are also shown in Table 5.4. The two chairmanships held by blacks were on D committees. It should be noted, however, that one fourth-termer, Mrs. DeVerne Calloway, did not receive her committee chairmanship until a vacancy was created by the death of Representative Frank C. Mazzuca, early in the legislative session. Representative Wayne P. Goode, who was originally assigned as the chairman of the Internal Affairs Committee, replaced Mazzuca as chairman of the Municipal Corporation Committee. Goode's place as head of the Internal Affairs Committee was assumed by Earl L. Sponsler. Sponsler had originally been assigned as chairman of the Federal-State Relations Committee. As a result of the musical-chairs reassignment of committee leadership positions, Mrs. Calloway emerged as the committee chairman for the rather unimportant committee on Federal-State Relations.

Besides the two committee chairmanships, members of the black delegation occupied roles of vice-chairmen on seven committees. Four of these were on C-ranked committees, with no positions being held on either the A or B committees. The vice-chairmen positions were held by Representative Ross (Public Health), Representative Holliday (Commerce), Representative Payne (Motor Vehicle), and Representative Goward (License). Representative Jordan served as vice-chairman of the D-ranked Employment Security Committee. Representatives Calloway and Johnson were given assignments as vice-chairmen on E-rated committees of Accounts, and Bills Perfected and Passed, respectively.

TABLE 5.4

RANKINGS OF COMMITTEES ON WHICH BLACK REPRESENTATIVES SERVED

Committees	Committee rankings	Number of Black committee members	Committee leadership positions held by Blacks[a]
Judiciary	A	1	
Government organization	A	1	
Education	A	1	
Local Government	A	1	
Fees and Salaries	A	1	
Appropriations	A	1	
Motor Vehicle	C	2	V-C (Payne)
Elections	C	2	
Municipal Corporations	C	3	
Public Health	C	1	V-C (Ross)
Insurance	C	1	
License	C	2	V-C (Goward)
Commerce	C	2	V-C (Holliday)
Labor	D	4	Chr. (Troupe)
Atomic Energy and Industrial Development	D	3	
Federal-State Relations	D	3	Chr. (Calloway)
Military and Veteran Affairs	D	2	

TABLE 5.4 (Continued)

Committees	Committee rankings	Number of Black committee members	Committee leadership positions held by Blacks[a]
Miscellaneous Resolutions	D	1	
Employment Security	D	2	V-C (Jordan)
Accounts	E	1	V-C (Calloway)
Bills Perfected and Passed	E	1	V-C (Johnson)

[a]V-C means vice-chairman and Chr. means chairman.

Source: The above was compiled from information in State of Missouri, House Journal, 75th General Assembly, Volume 1, Regular session, compiled by James C. Kirkpatrick, Secretary of State, pp. 2260-2349; and Official Manual State of Missouri, 1969-70 (Jefferson City, Missouri: James C. Kirkpatrick, Secretary of State, 1970), pp. 286-189.

In essence the black representatives held no positions of leadership on any of the major committees of the House. The total number of bill referrals to A- and B-ranked committees, where blacks held no positions of leadership, was 853 (65 percent of all referrals). The committees chaired by black representatives processed only nineteen bills or $1\frac{1}{2}$ percent of the total legislative measures referred to committees. The five functioning committees with black vice-chairmen were given a total of 135 bills or slightly more than 10 percent of all bill referrals.

Committee assignment scores

A more complete picture of the committee assignments given black members can be seen by evaluating their committee responsibilities. Each committee's responsibility has already been determined by the distribution of the legislative work load. To reiterate, this was accomplished by making general distinctions among the committees on the basis of the ideal bill-referral rate. By utilizing these committee work-load rankings it was possible to also produce a committee assignment score for each member of the legislature. Each committee assignment was given a numerical score--five points were given for an assignment to an A committee, four points for a B committee, three for a C, two for a D, and one for an E. An additional two points were given for those holding a committee chairmanship and one point for a vice-chairmanship. The legislator's committee assignment score was then calculated by totaling his appropriate points. An example: legislator A was appointed to the following committees: Appropriations (5 points), Public Health (3 points), and Education (5 points); assignment score, 13.

Before evaluating the blacks with reference to committee assignment scores, attention needs to be given to the role which seniority plays in the appointments. Although, unlike Congress, there is no seniority rule in the Missouri House, seniority was an important factor in the appointment of committee leadership and the assignment of members to committees. During the 75th General Assembly those members of the majority party who had served in at least the last three sessions of the House were given committee chairmanships. Those members beginning their third term in the House were generally assured of receiving a committee vice-chairmanship.

In order to facilitate the reporting of committee assignment scores, individual scores were grouped according to party and race with additional controls provided for the length of tenure in the House. By averaging the scores within each group, it was possible to obtain a group score for each category, as demonstrated in Table 5.5. Consistently, when controlling for seniority, the black members of the House had lower scores than their white counterparts of the majority party. The members of the Republican Party, as expected, had the lowest scores as a result of their minority status in the House. It is interesting to note that the interval between black Democrat scores and Republican scores was smaller than the interval between black Democrats and white Democrats for those who had served in the House less than four terms. The consistent difference between white and black Democrats in committee assignment scores is graphically illustrated in Figure 5.1.

Utilizing these data as the basis for determining responsibilities in committee assignments, it is possible to suggest that the observations made by Hadwiger in his earlier study of the Missouri House concerning the role of the Negro member and his committee assignments are still true today. With reference to committee assignments, Hadwiger reported, "It would appear that the nine Negroes who served in the House from 1947-56 were not considered equal to whites."[15] Where Negro members had obtained sufficient seniority to hold a committee chairmanship "the committees. . .met seldom, if at all, and ordinarily handled no important bills."[16]

TABLE 5.5

COMMITTEE ASSIGNMENT SCORES (CAS) [a] BY RACE, PARTY, AND TENURE

Tenure Categories	RACE AND PARTY CATEGORIES			
	All Dem-[b] ocrats	White[b] Democrats	Black Democrats	Republi- cans
1st Term				
Number of members	17	12	5	7
Average CAS	6.41	6.83	5.40	4.71
2nd Term				
Number of members	29	26	3	25
Average CAS	10.45	10.45	9.67	9.32
3rd Term				
Number of members	23	20	3	8
Average CAS	11.74	11.85	11.00	10.75
4th Term or more				
Number of members	37	35	2	14
Average CAS	11.84	11.86	11.50	9.64

[a]The Committee Assignment Score (CAS) was based upon the committee rankings by work load to which individual members were assigned. See Table 5.3 for explanation on committee rankings. The CAS was computed by assigning A committees 5 points, B committees 4 points, C committees 3 points, D committees 2 points, and E committees 1 point. A score was reached by totaling the points assigned to each committee for which the legislator was appointed. In order to show committee responsibility as accurately as possible, additional points were assigned to those members holding leadership positions on the committees: 2 points for a chairmanship and 1 point for a vice-chairmanship.

[b]This table does not include the three principal leaders of the House whose committee responsibilities were light as a result of their leadership positions (Speaker, Speaker Pro tempore, and Majority Floor Leader).

Source: The above was compiled from information cited in Table 5.3 on committee rankings and information on committee assignments in Official Manual State of Missouri, 1969-70 (Jefferson City, Missouri: James C. Kirkpatrick, Secretary of State, 1970), pp. 186-189.

FIGURE 5.1

A COMPARISON OF WHITE AND BLACK DEMOCRATS'
COMMITTEE ASSIGNMENT SCORES BY TENURE

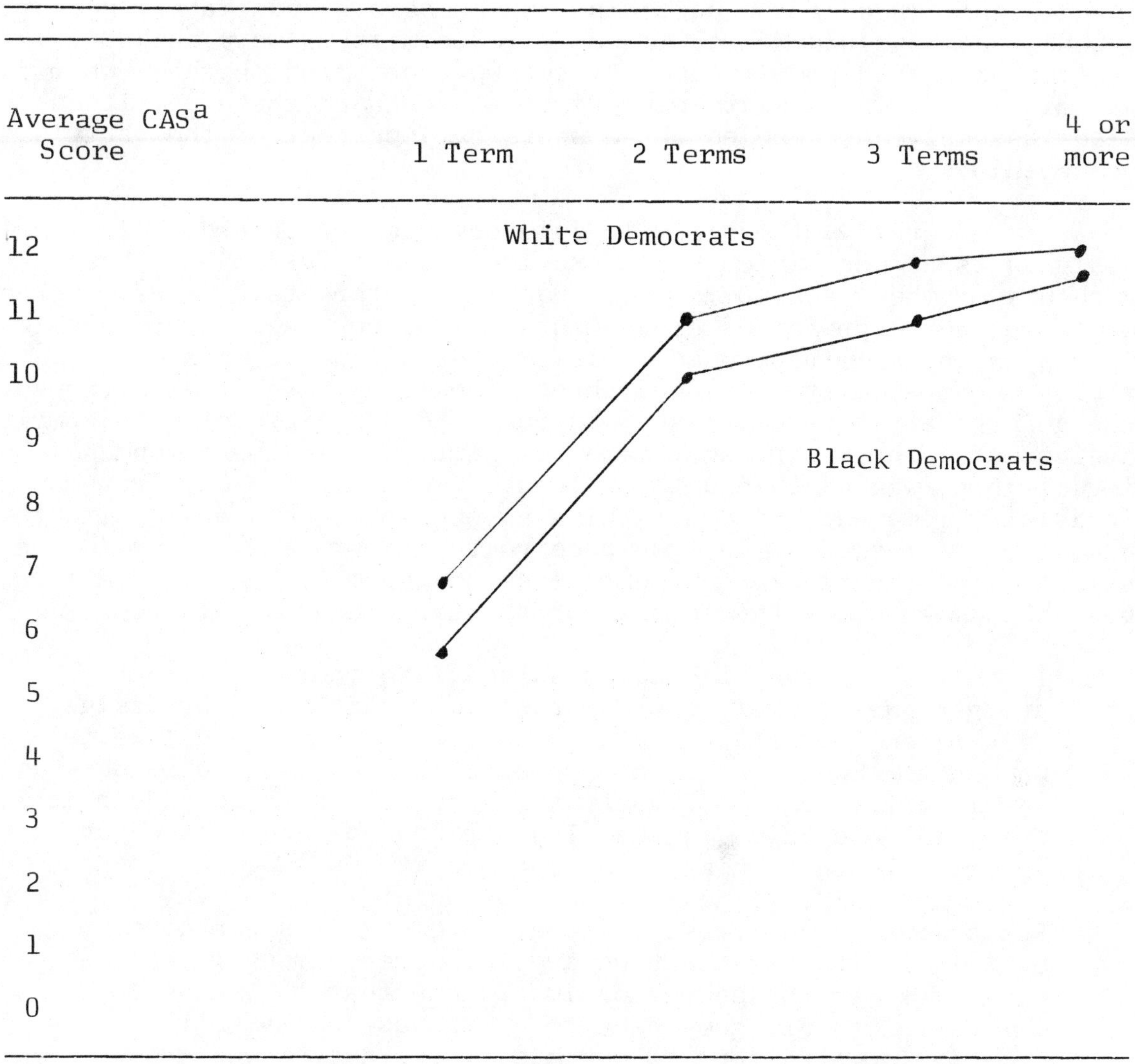

[a]CAS = Committee Assignment Score. See Table 5.5 for explanation.

Source: See Table 5.5 for explanation.

The black legislators' attitudes toward committee assignments

The consideration of committee assignments for black members of the House is incomplete without giving attention to the perceptions of black solons on committees which were most important to the needs of their constituents. Eleven of the Negro representatives identified

the committees they felt to be vital to their communies. Each
representative was permitted to name as many committees as he wished.
Two committees, as shown by Table 5.6, were mentioned by at least
half of those members: the Social Security and Retirement Committee
and the Education Committee. Three other committees were selected
by at least three of the participating members: Judiciary, Appropriations, and Ways and Means. These five committees were ranked
earlier as A or B committees. Black representation on these committees
was minimal. Of the sixty-nine Democrat seats on these committees,
black assemblymen occupied three seats or 4 percent of the party's
membership.

Generally, the black legislators did not regard their committee
assignments as ones which would provide a basis for solving the
problems of the black community. One legislator stated, "We have not
had some of the preferred assignments." Another legislator recalled,
"I was on one committee when I first entered /the legislature/. . .a
mickey mouse committee; it had three black people on it." Although
the general attitude expressed was one of disappointment with committee
assignments, there were some members, particularly the freshman
legislators, who explained their lack of enthusiasm. One freshman
legislator remarked, "I don't think anyone would be pleased with the
committee assignments that you receive the first time around." The
situation of the black representatives and committee assignments can
best be summed up by the remarks of a veteran Negro legislator.

> I don't think the blacks are spread into committees that
> are germane to their ghetto problems. . .it's not by design;
> each person makes a request of what he or she would like to
> be and the Speaker then attempts. . .to formulate his make-
> up of committees. . .I don't think he looked at the Education
> Committee and said, "Ah-ha, I don't have but one black person
> on it." I don't think he approached it that way; he looked
> at it and said, "I have so many Democrats and so many
> Republicans," and first he takes care of his supporters.
> So I think that the fact we are not spread among the
> committees to the degree of importance that they have to
> our districts all goes back to us because we haven't made
> any particular effort to do this. . .we just haven't
> scrutinized; except later when we get our assignments, we
> say we do not have this and we do not have that. . .It
> hasn't been a seriously tackled problem. . .We are taking it
> on as part of our proposal to get a better spread of
> representation on the committees that affect our districts.

TABLE 5.6

HOUSE COMMITTEES PERCEIVED BY BLACK REPRESENTATIVES
AS IMPORTANT TO THE NEGRO COMMUNITY

Committee		
Social Security and Retirement	8	B
Education	7	A
Judiciary	4	A
Appropriations	4	A
Ways and Means	3	B
Banking	2	C
Municipal Government	2	C
Insurance	1	C
Economics	1	A
Local Government	1	A
Employment Security	1	D
Atomic Energy and Industrial Development	1	D

aSee Table 5.3 for explanation of committee ranking.

Source: This information was tabulated from interviews held with the black representatives.

Summary

As an identifiable group in the Missouri House the black representatives have not been completely integrated into the organizational structure of the legislative body. This conclusion is founded upon an inquiry into the roles preferred by black solons within the organization of the Missouri lower chamber. Two distinct characteristics of the House's organizational structure were examined, leadership positions and the committee system.

Leadership roles performed by black members of the House were limited. For the purposes of this inquiry leadership positions were defined as being of two types, chamber and political party. The distinction between the two types was based upon (1) the primary orientation of the role and (2) the eligibility to hold a position. A chamber position had as its primary focus the performance of a task for the whole legislature, whereas a political party position was primarily oriented to the performance of some role for a sub-group of the legislature--the political party. Eligibility for assuming a leadership position differed for the two types. All members were potential candidates for a political party position. This, however, was not true for chamber positions, which were limited to members of the majority party.

All Negro representatives in the Missouri House during the period of 1969-70 affiliated with the Democratic Party. Since they were aligned with the majority party, they had access to the chamber positions: Speaker, Speaker pro tempore, committee chairman-ships, and committee vice-chairmanships. This situation increased immensely the opportunities for blacks to perform leadership roles, as there were forty standing committees. Two black representatives served as committee chairmen and seven as vice-chairmen. These were the only leadership positions held by black representatives. In essence, the black solons performed leadership roles of the chamber type as opposed to the political party type, and within the chamber type they held minor positions rather than those which could be defined as the major roles.

Much like the roles performed by blacks within the leadership positions of the House, the roles they performed within the committee system were also limited. This conclusion was supported by several facts related to the division of the legislative labor by committees. First, committees which were chaired or vice-chaired by black representatives were not considered to be committees of major importance. This is certainly true when reviewing the work-load factor (number of bills assigned to a committee). Secondly, when comparing the blacks with other members of the Democratic Party, the committee assignments and responsibilities received by blacks were consistently less with regard to work load, even when a control for seniority was introduced. Thirdly, blacks did not have significant representation on those committees which they perceived as being important to their constituents.

Notes

[1]Malcolm E. Jewell, The State Legislature (New York: Random House, 1969), pp. 37-44.

[2]All state legislative bodies, except those in Nebraska and Minnesota, are organized by political parties. Ibid., p. 12.

[3]Angus Campbell, Philip E. Converse, Warren E. Miller and Donald E. Stokes, The American Voter (New York: John Wiley and Sons, Inc., 1960), pp. 92-93.

[4]A 1970 report by Elmer E. Smith, Missouri State Republican Chairman, revealed that there were no Negro Republican officeholders, state or local, in Missouri. Kansas City Star, February 4, 1970, p. 1-2.

[5]Interview with James Troupe, November 24, 1970.

[6]Al Wallace, "Big City Shop Talk," St. Louis Argus, November 29, 1968, p. 3-B.

[7]William J. Keefe and Morris S. Ogul, The American Legislative Process (Englewood Cliffs, New Jersey: Prentice-Hall, Inc., 1964), p. 143.

[8]Woodrow Wilson, Congressional Government (New York: Meridian Books, 1956), p. 69, cited by Keefe and Ogul, op. cit., p. 139.

[9]Robert F. Karsch, The Standing Committees of the Missouri General Assembly (Columbia, Missouri: Bureau of Government Research of the University of Missouri, 1959), p. i.

[10]George D. Young, "The Role of Political Parties in the Missouri House of Representatives" (unpublished Ph.D. dissertation, University of Missouri, 1958), p. 22.

[11]Malcolm E. Jewell and Samuel C. Patterson, The Legislative Process in the United States (New York: Random House, 1966), pp. 209-210.

[12]Robert F. Karsch, The Standing Committees of the Missouri General Assembly, op. cit., pp. 21-22.

[13]Ibid., p. 21.

[14]A discussion on the importance of the Appropriations Committee, although it received only a limited number of bills, can be found in Karsch, The Standing Committees of the Missouri General Assembly, op. cit., pp. 21-22.

[15]Don F. Hadwiger, "Representation in the Missouri General Assembly," Missouri Law Review, XXIV (April, 1959), p. 185.

[16]Ibid.

CHAPTER VI

THE BLACK LEGISLATOR AND POLICY INITIATION

The primary function performed by a legislative body is to make laws for the society which it serves. A vital part of this process is the procedure by which proposed alternatives to current laws or creation of new rules and programs are brought before the deliberative body. As a member of the legislature, each representative has the authority to initiate (sponsor) policy considerations. Access to the process of proposing public policy changes, however, is not tantamount to the adoption of new public policies. Yet initation is important because the legislature will consider only those matters placed before it. As a collective group, the members of the legislature by their decisions as to which items to introduce or sponsor narrow the potential list of possible alternatives to a relatively manageable number.

This discussion of the black legislators' role in initiating new public policies by their sponsorship of legislation centers on three questions. First, what types of public policies were initiated by the black assemblymen? Secondly, how successful were the Negro representatives in obtaining the adoption of their initiated policies. Thirdly, how did the black lawmakers perceive policy initiation? From these inquiries a better understanding of the black legislator's public policy priorities and effectiveness as a molder of public policy should be attained.

Legislation Sponsored by Black
Representatives

During the 1969 regular session 1,033 bills or joint resolutions originated in the lower house of the General Assembly.[1] Of these, seventy were either sponsored or jointly sponsored by black members of the House.[2] This represents slightly less than seven percent of the total amount of legislation introduced. In terms of the amount of legislation introduced by black members, and their eight percent proportion of the House membership, there is only a minimal deviation from the expectation of an ideal ratio of bill introduction and the number of bills actually authored.

Legislation sponsored by black members of the Missouri House covered a wide range of topics. As one might expect, however, the

the bulk of this legislation pertained to problems in their constituency. The nature of black-sponsored bills might best be shown by grouping the seventy legislative bills into several categories, as shown by Table 6.1.

Legislation pertaining to state and local governmental units accounted for the largest category of bills sponsored by blacks. Most of the legislation was local in nature and was related to one of the political subdivisions in which Negro legislators resided. Nine bills directly pertained to some political subdivisions or its officials in Jackson County. The one local bill introduced by a black member for St. Louis related to compensation in the offices of Sheriff and Recorder of Deeds. One general local government bill would have provided additional funds for cities and counties by increasing the tax on cigarettes and distributing the funds on a per capita basis.

TABLE 6.1

BLACK-SPONSORED LEGISLATION BY CATEGORIES

Categories	Number of Bills
State and Local Government	15
Civil Rights	11
Consumer Protection	11
Welfare	8
Public Housing	7
Law Enforcement	6
Labor	5
Elections	3
Education	1
Miscellaneous	3
Total	70

Source: The above was compiled from information in State of Missouri, House Journal, 75th General Assembly, Volume 1, Regular session, compiled by James C. Kirkpatrick, Secretary of State, pp. 2372-2375, 2379-2424.

Two bills had a broader state interest than those related to local government. One would have eliminated the residency requirement for new members of the Highway Patrol. The other would have provided for special license plates for Missouri's Congressional Delegation.

Finally, two bills were significantly oriented toward Negro interest in the state political system. One bill called for a constitutional amendment permitting the state and its political subdivisions to grant or lend funds to private groups for community development. The sponsor viewed this bill as an attempt to get funds from the state to help build up inner-city areas. The other bill would have increased the compensation received by members of the Commission on Civil Rights. The author stated that it was his intention to compensate the members of this commission at the same rate received by members of other state commissions.

Generally, black representatives were serving requests made of them by officials of various political subdivisions or organizations when they sponsored state and local legislation. This is not an unusual practice for state legislators.

A policy area where it is commonly expected that Negro members would be active in sponsoring bills is civil rights. The black members of the Missouri House authored eleven bills which can be regarded as civil rights-oriented. Most of these were of minor importance considering the civil rights efforts of the 1960's. Three bills proposed eliminating the designation of race in voting registration. Two bills followed earlier Supreme Court rulings by repealing Missouri's laws prohibiting and providing a penalty for inter-racial marriages.[3] Two bills were sponsored with the intention of giving Missouri a fair housing law, although the federal government had previously legislated in this area of civil rights. One bill was introduced as an effort to broaden the fair employment laws of Missouri by prohibiting any employer from discriminating. Another attempted to regulate the cancelling of insurance policies on the basis of race. Requiring the teaching of Negro and other ethnic group history in Missouri schools was the content of one bill. Although not necessarily a civil rights act, one bill increased the membership on the State Board of Cosmetology. Its classification with civil rights legislation arises from the purpose for its intro-duction. The sponsor regarded the cosmetology business as the largest Negro business in the state. Its regulation board, the State Board of Cosmetology, had no black members. The representative had been assured by Governor Hearnes that this situation would be corrected if he could secure the passage of legislation increasing the board's membership.

Compared to actions taken by the federal government in recent years, the civil rights legislation sponsored by blacks in the Missouri House during the 1969 session was relatively mild. Of the legislation introduced, the bills on fair housing, fair employment, and the teaching of Negro history were the most salient. The remaining bills were of minor significance to the civil rights movement.

Generally, the overall emphasis of legislation sponsored by blacks was on correcting problems faced by those in the lower strata of society. Although this legislation would benefit those of all races in similar societal positions, there is little argument that the blacks, in general, would benefit greatly from the adoption of much of this legislation.

Eight bills were introduced in an effort to strengthen the welfare program for the recipients. The changes proposed by seven of these bills would have permitted recipients to have more intangible financial interests, to obtain additional housing allowances, and would have changed the mechanics of applying for and receiving welfare payments in such a manner as to benefit the destitute recipients. An additional welfare-related bill would have had the state assume additional responsibility for the support of poor people in the major metropolitan areas of the state.

Seven bills were introduced relating to the management of public housing authorities. Two bills attempted to establish a system of rental charge based upon the income of the renter. Two others called for state aid to the public housing authorities. One would have required officials of public housing authorities to meet with tenants for the purpose of discussing grievances, while another bill would have provided for the appointment of more tenants to the housing commission in St. Louis. Finally, one bill would have prohibited cities from realizing any revenue from their housing authorities.

As can be detected in some of the proposed legislation in the areas of welfare, public housing, and even in one of the civil rights bills, there was strong interest in consumer protection. The Negro legislators proposed several pieces of legislation which would hopefully give the consumer stronger protection from various business enterprises. Cancellation of insurance policies was the target of two bills. One would set out specific conditions under which automobile insurance could be cancelled. The other would create an insurance appeals board with the responsibility for determining the justification for cancelling insurance policies. Sellers of repossessed automobiles were the subject of a bill which would require them to give certain notices prior to seeking deficiency judgments. Another bill would allow the purchaser of an item sold by a door-to-door salesman to cancel the purchase within a certain period of time. One bill would require public utility companies to pay interest upon deposits as guantees of payment. One legislator sponsored a bill to regulate closing or going-out-of-business sales because he felt that many times they were presented to the consumer in such a manner as to be misleading. Lastly, a bill to define prepaid hospital and medical expense contracts as insurance was sponsored by a black representative.

Legislation related to non-public housing was directed at the protection of the renter from the landlord. One would require warrants of fitness in residential property leases, while another bill would require owners to deliver summons in landlord-tenant cases by certified mail. One bill would make it mandatory for those holding easement rights on a person's property to pay a portion of the costs of upkeep and repair. Another, oriented more toward safety, would require all trailers to have a minimum of two exits.

Since crime rates and convictions are commonly high in ghetto areas, it was not surprising to find several black-sponsored bills related to law enforcement. Four bills were introduced with provisions granting additional protection to the arrested person. Two of these would prohibit the disclosure of arrest records when no conviction resulted. Another would permit the use of a chauffeur's or operator's license for bail bond in traffic arrests. A fourth bill would repeal the right of the Board of Training Schools to transfer children to adult correctional institutions. An additional bill was designed to restore some freedom denied to the felon. It would have eliminated the permanent exclusion from voting for second felony convictions or for election offenses. Lastly, one bill was aimed at the sometimes criticized operations of local jails. This legislation would have established a division of jail service, which would assist political subdivisions with the operation of their jails, within the state Department of Corrections.

It was not surprising to find that the Negro lawmakers sponsored several bills on behalf of labor. This is especially true when considering the labor background of several black House members and the rather large proportion of blacks in blue-collar jobs. Of the five bills relating to labor, three of these dealt with the discharge of employees. One would provide that an employee discharged because his salary had been garnisheed could recover for damages. Another would give any employee discharged or discriminated against the power of action against the employer. The third bill would require employers to pay an employee his wages upon termination or continue to pay him as a penalty. Another bill would have affected the state government by requiring bi-monthly payments to state employees. A bill to change the qualifications for obtaining a barber's license was introduced so that former criminals who were trained in the profession could obtain the necessary license. The sponsor remarked that under present regulations many were rejected for failing to meet a high moral qualification.

Education has been mentioned by the black legislators as one of the major concerns in the Negro community. One bill was authored by a Negro representative with the intent of establishing aid for underprivileged students who go to college. The best method for escaping the conditions of poverty is to acquire the skills and the training which can provide the basis for earning adequate wages. Since it is difficult for those in poverty to finance the cost of higher education, the essence of this legislation was to have the state assume a share of the expenses.

Of the remaining legislation introduced by the group under study, three bills focused on elections. One of the several bills to provide for a presidential primary in the state was authored by a black. A second bill would require voter registration drives at least three times a year in counties having Boards of Election Commissioners. Both of the foregoing bills could have increased the level of black participation in the electoral process. A change in the date of school board elections in Kansas City was the subject of a third bill.

Three bills sponsored by black solons defied classification in the above categories and as a result were labeled miscellaneous. One would provide for a severance tax on certain minerals, natural resources, and their products. The financing of veteran bonuses by interest accumulated on state monies on time deposits was the provision of a second bill. A third bill proposed a change in the permissible motor vehicle lengths and widths of trucks on state highways.

Success of Black-Sponsored Legislation

Having outlined the types of legislation sponsored by the Negro members of the House in the previous section, it is now appropriate to inquire into the success of the black members in maneuvering their bills through the lawmaking maze. Sixteen, nearly one quarter of the seventy legislative bills introduced by the black members, were successful in the lower house. Six of the sixteen eventually passed the Senate and were approved by the Governor. None of the black-sponsored bills which passed both houses were vetoed by the Governor. Thus less than 9 percent of the total number of bills introduced by black members of the House succeeded in hurdling all the obstacles in the legislative process.

What significance, if any, can be attached to the degree of success achieved by black representatives in obtaining desired policy outputs? This inquiry may be answered by having some indication as to the proportion of success which might normally be expected. In a relative format, was Negro-sponsored legislation less successful than that sponsored by the House membership as a whole and other legislative groups? For the 1969 regular session of the Missouri House the success ratio of all bills passed in the House (368) to all bills introduced (1033) was 36 percent. Non-black members achieved 37 percent success for their sponsored legislation (341 out of 963 bills). Negro members of the House had only a 22.9 percent record (see Table 6.2).

The same analysis was applied to the proportion of bills referred to the State Senate and the successful passage of legislation in that chamber. Once again the bills authored by the black House members fell short of the norm, as shown in Table 6.3.

TABLE 6.2

SUCCESS OF HOUSE-INITIATED LEGISLATION IN THE HOUSE

Sponsors of legislation	Number of legislative items introduced[a]	Number of items passed by the House	Percentage of items passed by House
All members	1033	368	35.6
Non-black members	963	352	36.6
Black members	70	16	22.9

[a]Includes all House Bills and Joint Resolutions

Source: The above information was tabulated from State of Missouri, House Journal, 75th General Assembly, Volume 1, Regular session, compiled by James C. Kirkpatrick, Secretary of State, pp. 2260-2319, 2345-2348.

TABLE 6.3

SUCCESS OF HOUSE-INITIATED LEGISLATION IN THE SENATE

Sponsors of legislative items	Number of House legislative items sent to Senate	Number of House legislative items passed by Senate	Percentage of items passed by Senate
All members	368	174	47.3
Non-black members	352	168	47.7
Black members	16	6	37.5

Source: The above information was tabulated from State of Missouri, House Journal, 75th General Assembly, Volume 1, Regular session, compiled by James C. Kirkpatrick, Secretary of State, pp. 2260-2319, 2345-2348.

Success and legislative topic

To understand further the lesser success of Negro assemblymen compared to the greater success of white members of the lower chamber, it might prove helpful to examine the types of bills sponsored by blacks which did manage to obtain approval in at least one of the legislative chambers. Negro-sponsored legislation in the areas of civil rights and state and local government achieved the highest rates of success. Of the sixteen bills receiving favorable House action, six were on civil rights, five on state and local government, one on law enforcement, two on elections, and two on labor. Senate approval was obtained for two civil rights bills, three state and local government bills, and one election bill.

An evaluation of successful legislation

Accomplishments made by black members in the Missouri House, with reference to the success they achieved in securing the passage of the bills they introduced, were not of the highest degree of importance. This conclusion is evident when comparing the nature of the bills winning legislative approval with those that did not. Negro-sponsored legislation related to the social-economic concerns of the black community failed to obtain the necessary support in the House, as demonstrated in Table 6.4. None of the twenty-seven bills classified in the areas of consumer protection, welfare, public housing, and education received favorable action from the House.

This is not meant to indicate, however, that all black-sponsored bills which passed the House were of minor importance. Several bills which passed the House were viewed as important by the Negro members. Most prominent of these were the bills related to the teaching of Negro and other ethnic group history in state schools; to the establishment of prohibitions against employment discrimination; to the interdictions against auto insurance discrimination on the basis of race, color, or creed; and to the restrictions prohibiting law enforcement agencies from disclosing arrest records which did not eventuate in convictions.

While a few bills of major importance passed the House, none of them received the necessary support to pass the State Senate. Of the six bills which did manage to maneuver successfully through both houses of the legislature none can be referred to as being of major importance to the black community. Two of these merely went through the motions of conforming to earlier Supreme Court rulings which had declared as void state laws which prohibited the marriage between persons of different races. Other successful bills made minor contributions by changing the three-year residency requirement needed for appointment to the state highway patrol, changing the date of the school board elections in Kansas City, and increasing the salary of the Jackson County Circuit Clerk. The one bill that appeared to provide a new law which could have an impact on the black community, or a segment of the black community, was the bill that increased the

TABLE 6.4

SUCCESS OF BLACK-SPONSORED LEGISLATION BY ISSUE CATEGORIES

Issue categories	Number of sponsored legislative items	Number of items passed by House	Number of items passed by both House and Senate
State and Local Government	15	5	2
Civil Rights	11	6	3
Consumer Protection	11	0	0
Welfare	8	0	0
Public Housing	7	0	0
Law Enforcement	6	1	0
Labor	5	2	0
Elections	3	2	1
Education	1	0	0
Miscellaneous	3	0	0
Total	70	16	6

Source: The above information was tabulated from State of Missouri, House Journal, 75th General Assembly, Volume 1, Regular session, compiled by James C. Kirkpatrick, Secretary of State, pp. 2260-2319, 2345-2348.

number of members on the State Board of Cosmetology. It was reported earlier in this chapter that this bill was an effort to make possible the appointment of a black person to the board.

Status of legislative items at end of session

Having noted in the earlier discussion that legislation sponsored by Negro members of the House tended to lack the same success ratio as legislation sponsored by non-black members of the legislature, it is appropriate to ascertain, if possible, the point

in the legislative process at which the black-sponsored bills were
defeated. Most of the bills sponsored by black representatives were
never reported out of committee, as seen in Table 6.5. Favorable
committee action was obtained most often for legislation classified
as civil rights, law enforcement, and elections, while legislative
issues in the areas of consumer protection, welfare, public housing,
and education rarely received positive committee review. Thirty-
nine bills died simply by pigeonholing; three were sentenced to death
by the report "do not pass"; twelve were either stricken from the
calendar, tabled, or defeated on the House floor, after having
obtained positive committee reports.

Whether the status of Negro-sponsored bills at the end of
the legislative session was normal, can only be gauged by comparing
their status with that of other legislative bills. The same formula
for determining the success ratio of black-authored bills as against
the overall pattern of all the bills introduced in the same legislative
session, shown by Table 6.6, shows two major deviations for black-
sponsored legislation: legislation sponsored by black members of the
House had a higher rate of death by standing committee inaction, and,
as shown earlier, a lower level of success in obtaining House and
Senate approval. The remaining categories illustrated only minor
deviations.

TABLE 6.5

STATUS OF BLACK-SPONSORED LEGISLATION AT THE END OF THE REGULAR
HOUSE SESSION BY ISSUE CATEGORIES

Issue Category	Total number of legislative items	No committee report	Committee report do not pass	Stricken from the Calendar	Tabled	Defeated	Passed House; not Senate	Passed House and Senate
State & Local Government	15	6	1	2	1	0	2	3
Civil Rights	11	4	0	1	0	0	4	2
Consumer Protection	11	10	0	1	0	0	0	0
Welfare	8	8	0	0	0	0	0	0
Public Housing	7	5	0	1	0	1	0	0
Law Enforcement	6	2	0	1	0	2	1	0
Labor	5	1	1	1	0	0	2	0
Elections	3	0	0	0	0	1	1[a]	1
Education	1	1	0	0	0	0	0	0

TABLE 6.5 (Continued)

Issue Category	Total number of legislative items	No committee report	Committee report do not pass	Stricken from the calendar	Tabled	Defeated	Passed House; not Senate	Passed House and Senate
Miscellaneous	3	2	1	0	0	0	0	0
Total	70	39	3	7	1	4	10	6
Percentage	100%	56%	4%	10%	1%	6%	14%	9%

[a]HB 224 co-sponsored by Representative Ross was combined with HB 111 by a House committee substitute.

Source: State of Missouri, House Journal, 75th General Assembly, Volume 1, Regular session, compiled by James C. Kirkpatrick, Secretary of State, pp. 2260-2319, 2345-2348.

TABLE 6.6

STATUS OF HOUSE BILLS AND JOINT RESOLUTIONS
AT END OF REGULAR HOUSE SESSION

Status of legislative items	Black sponsored legislation	Non-black sponsored legislation	All legislation
No committee referral	0 (0%)	4 (a)	4 (a)
No committee report	39 (56%)	375 (39%)	414 (40%)
Committee report- do not pass	3 (4%)	49 (5%)	52 (5%)
Stricken	7 (10%)	154 (16%)	16 (16%)
Tabled	1 (1%)	4 (a)	5 (a)
Defeated on floor	4 (6%)	27 (3%)	31 (3%)
Passed House, but did not pass Senate	10 (14%)	182 (19%)	192 (19%)
Passed House and Senate	6 (9%)	168 (17%)	174 (17%)
Total	70 (100%)	963 (99%)	1033 (100%)

[a]less than 1%

Source: The above information was tabulated from State of Missouri, House Journal, 75th General Assembly, Volume 1, Regular session, compiled by James C. Kirkpatrick, Secretary of State, pp. 2260-2319, 2345-2348.

Committee composition and the success of legislation

As a result of the previous findings that bills authored by black members of the House were less successful in hurdling the committee obstacles than bills authored by non-black members, an inquiry into the committee structure as an explanation for this phenomenon appears to be appropriate. Is there a relationship between the committee's racial composition and its action on bills?

The question can be answered in the affirmative as shown by
Table 6.7. The racial composition of committees reviewing bills
sponsored by black members was related to the proportion of bills
given favorable recommendations by the standing committees. When
bills were referred to committees where a black legislator held one
of the two formal leadership positions, either chairman or vice-
chairman, the committee reported the bill favorably nearly 78 percent
of the time. In committees which included at least one black
representative, but no black occupant of the formal leadership
positions, bills received a favorable report on 45 percent of the
referrals. Bills authored by black members received the least
favorable committee action when there were no black members on the
committee, receiving favorable action on only 19 percent of the
referrals. The proportion of favorable committee actions increased
as the number of black members on a committee increased. Where one
black held a seat on a committee, favorable action was achieved on
43 percent of the referrals; where there were two black members,
favorable action increased to 57 percent; and where blacks held more
than two seats on the committee the action was 71 percent favorable.

Sponsor's seniority and success of legislation

In considering the factors related to the successful sponsorship of legislation, seniority is seen as one of the variables, as
exhibited in Table 6.8.

It is not surprising to find that the Negro freshman
representatives were less successful in acquiring passage of their
sponsored legislation than were those Negro lawmakers who had served
in previous General Assemblies. In comparison with non-black
representatives, the non-freshman black assemblymen were less successful
in sponsoring legislation; however, the same conclusions regarding
black and non-black freshman legislators cannot be as confidently
supported (see footnote a to Table 6.8).

Perceptions of Black Representatives on Policy
Initiation and the Success of Sponsored
Legislation

The discussion has focused on the role of black lawmakers
in sponsoring legislation considered by the Missouri General Assembly
and on the success variable for those legislative items. Rather
than abandon the discussion with the data collected from the records
of the Missouri House of Representatives, an examination of the
perceptions held by black solons on their sponsored legislation seems
appropriate. From the questionnaires and interviews administered
to the Negro representatives, two attitudes were expressed which
relate to the sponsorship and success of legislation.

First, as previous material in this chapter would suggest,
the black representatives viewed economic-related issues as the
areas of public policy which needed the greatest legislative attention.

TABLE 6.7

RACIAL COMPOSITION OF COMMITTEES AND FAVORABLE COMMITTEE
ACTION ON BLACK-SPONSORED LEGISLATION

Role of black members on the committees	Number of[a] legislation referrals	Number of fav-[b] orable committee reports	Percent- age
Held leadership position (chairman, vice-chairman)	9	7	77.8
One or more black members, but no leadership position	42	19	45.2
No black members	21	4	19.0
Number of blacks on committee			
0	21	4	19.0
1	30	13	43.3
2	14	8	57.1
more than 2	7	5	71.4

[a]Total number of referrals (72) is greater than the number of legislative items (70) as a result of bills involving new financial expenditures for the state being referred to both a substantive committee and the Economics Committee.

[b]A favorable committee report is defined as a "do pass" recommendation.

Source: The above information was tabulated from State of Missouri, House Journal, 75th General Assembly, Volume 1, Regular session, compiled by James C. Kirkpatrick, Secretary of State, pp. 2260-2319, 2345-2348.

TABLE 6.8

SENIORITY AND RACE FACTORS IN THE SUCCESS
OF SPONSORED LEGISLATION

Black members	Number of spon- sored legis- lative items	Number of leg- islative items passed by House	Percent- age
Freshman legislators	20[a]	2	10.0
Non-freshman legislators	50	14	28.0
Non-black members			
Freshman legislators	64[a]	10	15.6
Non-freshman legislators	899	342	38.5

[a]Legislation with joint sponsors where one sponsor was a freshman and the others non-freshmen was classified as a freshman bill. This occurred twice with black members and nineteen times with non-black members. Neither of the black freshmen who sponsored successful legislation had co-sponsors; however, seven of the ten successful bills by non-black freshmen had joint sponsorship with a senior member. By eliminating the co-sponsored bills the black freshmen would have successfully sponsored two of eighteen bills (11%) and the non-black freshmen would have successfully sponsored three of forty-five bills (7%)

Source: The above information was tabulated from State of Missouri, House Journal, 75th General Assembly, Volume 1, Regular session, compiled by James C. Kirkpatrick, Secretary of State, pp. 2260-2319, 2345-2348. ◂

Only four of the ten responding legislators viewed civil rights legislation as a primary concern in the passage of new state laws. Those who did give prominence to civil rights guarded their views by noting that such legislation was important only with regard to the establishment of a state law for fair housing and the need to strengthen the state's fair employment laws. Beyond these two civil rights concerns, it was economic improvement, welfare, and education that were perceived as the major legislative concerns of the Negro community. This corresponds with the emphasis placed upon socio-economic matters in legislation sponsored by blacks in the 75th General Assembly.

Secondly, material presented earlier in this chapter suggested that Negro-sponsored legislation was less likely to be successful in surviving the obstacles found in the legislative arena, compared with legislation sponsored by non-black members of the legislature. While this conclusion may be drawn by outsiders from the information presented, the black legislator himself did not generally perceive this as true. In responding to a question asking if they thought legislation sponsored by Negroes had the same chance of success as did legislation sponsored by non-black legislators, the black assemblymen generally agreed that the chance of success was the same for both. Seven of the nine Negro House members who responded to this question saw no difference. Two black freshman legislators strongly disagreed. Their disagreement might have been the result of the additional difficulties experienced by first-term legislators in securing the passage of legislation.

Summary

In the review of legislation authored by members of the black delegation in the Missouri House, it is clear that the emphasis of their legislative actions is heavily influenced by the nature of their constituency. Whereas lawmaking in the area of civil rights has been the common focus in recent years, the interest during the 1969 Missouri General Assembly was oriented more toward the general social-economic problems of the cities' ghettos. The concerns and goals of the Negro legislator--both in the articulation of priorities and in the operationalization of these priorities by sponsoring legislation--centered on the substantive areas of economics, welfare, housing, law enforcement, and education. The transformation of the primary policy orientations away from civil rights legislation to more general social-economic legislation resulted from the situation in which racial legal equality had advanced by this time to a point where it was no longer the major concern, at least as seen by the black representatives.

Since the initiation of legislative proposals is not equivalent to policy change, it was necessary to examine the successes and failures of black-sponsored legislation. This investigation produced several findings. First, black House members as compared with non-blacks were less likely to obtain either in the House or in both chambers approval for legislation which they sponsored as compared to non-black members. Secondly, the legislation which did successfully pass the House or both chambers did not include the more important black-sponsored items. Thirdly, the standing committee system was the point in the legislative process where most black-sponsored bills failed in the House. Proportionately more black-sponsored bills than non-black sponsored bills were defeated by the committees. This was particularly true when Negro legislators held no positions or only limited positions on the committee reviewing the bills.

[1]The material discussed in this section was compiled from information in State of Missouri, House Journal, 75th General Assembly, Volume 1, Regular session, compiled by James C. Kirkpatrick, Secretary of State, pp. 2260-2319, 2345-2348, 2373-2375, 2379-2424. Additional information was secured through interviews with twelve of the black representatives and by newspaper articles where they were applicable.

[2]For the purposes of this study, legislation identified as being sponsored by Negro members of the Missouri House was defined as any bill where: (1) a black representative was the sole sponsor of a bill (eleven bills); (2) two black representatives co-sponsored a bill (three bills); (3) the principal sponsor listed for a bill, when there were several co-sponsors, was a black representative (forty-six bills); and (4) a black representative co-sponsored a bill with a non-black colleague (ten bills). Sponsorship of a bill was determined by the listings of bill authors in State of Missouri, House Journal.

[3]Loving v. Virginia, 388 U.S. 1; 87 S. Ct. 1817; 18 L. Ed. 2d 1010 (1967).

CHAPTER VII

THE BLACK LEGISLATOR AND ROLL-CALL VOTING

The process of formulating public policy by a legislative body is affected by numerous factors. Two of these have been discussed: (1) the initiation of policy alternatives, as demonstrated by the legislative items placed before the deliberative body for consideration by legislator sponsorship, and (2) the procedure whereby policy alternatives are considered and recommendations are made on the proposed policies--specifically, the role performed by the standing committees. There is yet a third factor, the participation of the membership in voting on proposed policies when they are placed before the total legislative body for review and action. In essence, the concern now turns to the roll-call voting patterns of the black assemblymen.

Legislative voting behavior is considered by examining three related concerns. The style of collective voting patterns for the Negro House membership is the initial concern. A second concern directs attention to the impact which Negro representatives have on the policy output of the House as indicated by the decisions rendered on roll-call votes. Thirdly, attention is given to the actual participation or non-participation of the black membership in the roll-call votes.

Legislative Voting Patterns of
Black Representatives

As a minority group within the legislature, as well as within the larger society, and as a result of their recruitment from constituencies which share the same racial heritage and basic social-economic conditions, the black representatives would generally have common interests in legislative issues. From this premise the voting behavior exhibited by the Negro legislators in the 1969 session of the Missouri House was examined. After describing the selection of roll calls utilized in this study, and the method used in defining group cohesion, the Rice Index of Cohesion, group cohesion of the black solons will be analyzed. Once the cohesive nature of the black delegation in the Missouri lower chamber is established, a discussion of the differences in voting patterns between urban black and non-black representatives will be undertaken to locate legislative issues where the Negro representatives have different orientations than their party colleagues from the urban areas. Black legislators' voting patterns on issues sponsored by their Negro colleagues and on roll calls reflecting political party support will conclude this section.

Selection of roll-call votes

During the regular session of the 75th Missouri General Assembly the House recorded 1,047 roll-call votes.[1] In order to make the task of this research manageable, 213 of those votes were selected for review and inclusion in the effort to understand black legislative voting patterns.

The criteria followed in making the selection of these votes included the elimination of all roll-call votes where less than 10 percent of the total membership voted on one side of the issue. This step eliminated 538 roll calls where fewer than sixteen members voted opposite the majority. The primary justification for their exclusion was the premise that these votes did not reflect conflict situations in House voting. Since these votes represented relatively high cohesion levels for the House, there was little value in examining them.

From the remaining 509 roll calls the sample was chosen by selecting those votes which the researcher viewed as important to the urban areas of the state. Implicit in the definition of urban is the relevance of legislation to the black community.

Since most bills are likely to have some impact on the urban areas, the major exception being those legislative bills related to local governments in the non-urban areas, it is probable that several bills omitted from the sample involved issues which were pertinent to the urban areas. In essence, the reason for a vote's inclusion, rather than its exclusion was the degree of importance perceived by the researcher. Those roll calls viewed as having a greater importance to the urban areas were included while those votes seen as being of marginal importance were excluded. A sample of the types of issues excluded are the following bills by their short titles: H.B. 30 "Puts county assessors on salary and abolishes fee," H.B. 221 "Repeal sections relating to bounties on wild animals," and H.B. 317 "Statewide voter registration except in counties with board of election commissioners." Some errors in the selection are acknowledged as possible. The rather high portion of votes selected from the possible aggregate of conflict votes, however, should be sufficient to off-set any fallacy or misinterpretation. The selected sample represents 42 percent of the roll calls where conflict ran above 10 percent.

Rice Index of Cohesion

Adopted as a research tool for the purpose of locating group cohesion was the Rice Index of Cohesion. The Index of Cohesion, developed by Stuart Rice, provided a measure for testing unison in voting.[2] Rice's Index considers the relationship of positive and negative votes cast by a group on a given roll call or combination of roll-call votes. The formula can be stated as: percentage of yes votes minus percentage of negative votes times 100 equals Index of Cohesion.[3] The formula does not take into consideration the members of the group who did not vote on the given issue. This is appropriate since it is difficult to conjecture as to why certain members failed to vote on the issue and how they would have voted if they had been present and voted. On the Rice Index of Cohesion a score of 100 represents complete group unity, those situations where all members of the group voted alike, and a score of 0 is tantamount to a conflict situation where the group's votes were divided equally between the ayes and the noes. The higher the Index score the greater the unity among the members of a given group.

Cohesion of black legislators on roll-call voting

Cohesion on roll-call voting among the members of the black House delegation was relatively high during the 1969 session. The Negro representatives were completely cohesive in their voting on 40 percent of the sampled roll calls. High levels of conflict, where the delegation equally divided its votes on a roll call (Index scores of 0), were limited to 2 percent of the votes reviewed. On 75 percent of the individual votes the black delegation had Index scores of 50.0 or higher. Their average Rice Index score for the 213 roll calls was 69.3.

At this juncture, the sum of our knowledge of Negro voting patterns is that as a group they did vote relatively cohesively on legislative roll calls. But there is no measure which indicates the uniqueness of the black delegation's voting behavior. In order to provide such a tool, voting patterns for white Democrat legislators from the two urban areas were examined. Under the assumption that white Democrat urban legislators would generally share the same basic legislative interests as blacks, the white Democrats were established as a control group. A comparison of the cohesion scores for each group shows that they are both equally cohesive. White urban Democrats averaged 69.9 on the Rice Index as compared to the black score of 69.3. As a result, this researcher concluded that the general level of black group cohesion is not unique and certainly could not be attributed to a consciousness of ethnic heritage or the ethnicity of his constituency.

The analysis of group cohesion needs further development to determine if substantive areas produce higher scores for the blacks as compared with the non-blacks. To carry out this task, the 213 roll calls were sub-divided into twelve issue categories. Results from this comparison, as shown in Table 7.1, did not demonstrate any major deviations from the earlier conclusions of similarity in group cohesion. Only two issue categories showed deviations which were greater than 10 points on the Rice Index. Black cohesion was substantially higher in the areas of civil rights and law enforcement legislation. Deviation in cohesion scores between blacks and non-blacks might be explained by the importance of these two issues to the black community. It was not surprising to find that blacks were in absolute agreement on civil rights issues. In the second area, law enforcement, blacks were likely to be more sensitive to procedural and institutional conditions of law enforcement than are representatives of the white community. The deviation in scores on the other issue categories was minimal at best and did not show substantial deviations in group cohesion.

TABLE 7.1

COHESION SCORES[a] FOR URBAN DEMOCRAT LEGISLATORS IN THE
MISSOURI HOUSE ON SELECTED ROLL CALLS

Legislative Issue Category	Number of Roll Calls	Cohesion Scores for Black members[b]	Cohesion Scores for Non-black members	Difference
Law Enforcement	19	84.8	54.1	-30.7
Civil Rights	3	100.0	88.0	-12.0
St. Louis oriented	35	69.5	78.1	-8.6
Labor	13	82.6	90.7	-8.1
Public Interest (Consumer Protection)	23	41.8	48.1	-6.3
Kansas City oriented	29	54.0	59.2	-5.2
Health and Welfare	8	72.2	75.2	-3.0
General Local Government	8	91.8	94.7	-2.9
Housing	11	84.1	81.9	-2.2
Education	21	68.2	68.8	-.6
Taxation	33	70.7	71.2	-.5

TABLE 7.1 (Continued)

COHESION SCORES[a] FOR URBAN DEMOCRAT LEGISLATORS IN THE
MISSOURI HOUSE ON SELECTED ROLL CALLS

Legislative Issue Category	Number of Roll Calls	Cohesion Scores for Black members[b]	Cohesion Scores for Non-black members	Difference
Congressional Redistricting	10	81.7	81.6	-.1
Total	213	69.3	69.9	-.6

[a]Cohesion scores are defined by the following formula:

$$\frac{\text{"Aye" votes} - \text{"No" votes}}{\text{"Aye" votes} + \text{"No" votes}} \times 100 = \text{Cohesion Score}$$

Absolute cohesion is found when all members of a group vote alike on a roll call, or when the cohesion score is 100.0. Group cohesion decreases as the score declines toward the point where the group's members are equally divided on a roll call, or where the score is 0.

[b]The cohesion scores presented represent an average of the group's scores on the individual roll calls.

Source: State of Missouri, House Journal, 75th General Assembly, Volume 1, Regular session, compiled by James C. Kirkpatrick, Secretary of State.

Index of Likeness

Thus far, our attention has been directed at group cohesion. The Rice Index of Cohesion scores show the nature of intra-group voting patterns, but are deficient in demonstrating inter-group voting patterns. Voting similarity within the membership of the urban group has been established as being relatively high for blacks and non-blacks, with each group having basically the same level of group member support. The more important question that needs attention is whether the blacks and non-blacks were acting in harmony or in conflict when voting on issues.

Should inter-group differences exist between the racial sub-groups of the urban delegations, it might be possible to illustrate areas of legislative policy-making where racial origins did contribute to legislative behavior. Adopted as a research mechanism for showing inter-group conflict was the Index of Likeness.[4] By examining the proportional frequency of group members voting "Aye" on roll calls and comparing each group's frequency, it is possible to demonstrate the degree of difference between two groups.[5] Because it demonstrates the degree of likeness in voting, the Index of Likeness is preferred to methods which simply locate the votes when the majority of one group opposes the majority of another group.

Difference in voting patterns between black and non-black urban Democrats

In applying the Index of Likeness to the legislative roll calls, the purpose is to show those areas where the two groups differed in their voting patterns. On the Likeness Index a score of 0 represents absolute dissimilarity in the groups on a roll call, and a score of 100 indicates the maximum level of inter-group voting similarity. Thus, the lower the score on the Likeness Index, the larger the deviation of the two groups in their voting patterns on a roll call. The Likeness Index average for the 213 votes examined was 81.9. Although it shows signs of some dissimilarity, it is rather minimal. On the whole, one could conclude that a low level of inter-group conflict existed between the urban white Democrat and the black Democrat. In applying the Likeness Index to categoric substantive areas of legislation, there were only two issue areas which showed signs of relatively strong group disagreement, as demonstrated by Table 7.2, law enforcement and education. To a lesser extent conflict above the average level was also found in the areas of taxation and public interest legislation.

It is possible to hypothesize that where voting pattern differences did exist, they were the result of different legislative orientations. A solon's orientation toward issues is at least partially, if not completely, a product of the constituency he represents. This suggests that the black assemblyman's basically Negro constituency has certain needs and interests which require him to vote differently from other urban legislators on certain types of legislation. Differences between these two groups, in their voting behavior on certain issues, can be illustrated by examining a sample of the roll calls where conflict was the highest.

In the category of law enforcement is a legislative issue commonly referred to as the Public Defender Bill. In discussing the current situation in Missouri, Representative Holliday reported:

> None of the existing systems. . .fully protects the interest of the accused in all areas and at all stages of the prosecution as required by the recent decisions of the U.S. Supreme Court. As a consequence, many persons accused of crimes in this state are convicted, but later released on a showing of inadequate legal representation. The Public Defender Bill proposes to close this loophole. Under this bill the Public Defender is obliged to represent an indigent accused as soon

TABLE 7.2

INDEX OF LIKENESS SCORES[a] FOR URBAN DEMOCRAT LEGISLATORS
OF THE MISSOURI HOUSE ON SELECTED ROLL CALLS

Legislative Issue Category	Number of votes	Index of Likeness Scores[b]
Civil Rights	3	94.0
Housing	11	93.6
General Local Government	8	93.2
Congressional Redistricting	10	93.0
Labor	13	89.8
St. Louis oriented	35	87.4
Health and Welfare	8	82.6
Kansas City oriented	29	81.2
Public Interest (Consumer Protection)	23	80.8
Taxation	33	78.9
Education	21	70.9
Law Enforcement	19	67.2
Total	213	81.9

[a]Index of Likeness scores are defined by the following
formula:
100- (% of Group A voting "Aye" - % of Group B voting "Aye") =
Index of Likeness
Complete similarity in group voting is represented by 100
and complete dissimilarity in group voting is represented by 0.

[b]The Likeness scores presented are an average of the scores
on the individual roll calls.

Source: State of Missouri, House Journal, 75th General
Assembly, Volume 1, Regular session, compiled by James C. Kirkpatrick,
Secretary of State.

as he is arrested and through all of the proceedings. It
has been estimated that 80 to 90 percent of the persons
accused of a crime are indigent; and are unable to hire
an attorney. The Public Defender under this bill will
be obligated to represent these people.[6]

The Public Defender Bill and the Pre-Arraignment Code Bill
which "spells out the procedure which police and prosecutor must
follow when a person is arrested and suspected or charged with having
committed a crime"[7] were two of the bills where conflict was found
between Negro solons and the urban white Democrat legislators.
Although Representative Holliday did not explicitly identify these
as salient issues to the Negro community, the inference is clear.
The indigent position of many Negroes, certainly a higher proportion
when compared with the non-black population, makes these issues
particularly salient to the black community.

In addition, high levels of disagreement were recorded on
roll calls related to correctional institutions, which were classified
under the law enforcement issue category. These bills called for
restrictions on transferring juveniles from the state training school
to adult penal institutions, providing for prison furloughs and the
establishment of a division of jail services in the state corrections
department which would assist political sub-divisions in the state
in the operation of their correctional institutions. It was not
surprising to find a difference between black and non-black urban
Democrats, considering the impact of these issues on the constituencies represented by each group.

Two different issues provided the basic cause for relatively
higher conflict between urban blacks and white Democrats on education
roll calls. State aid to local school districts became the fundamental
issue when the legislature:

> recognized for the first time that the cost of educating the
> socially and economically disadvantaged is greater than the
> cost of educating others, and urban districts with large
> numbers of disadvantaged children are to be given more money
> than other districts.[8]

Another area of state aid produced conflict when a bill providing
vocational or technical training assistance to children, from families
receiving Aid to Dependent Children, was considered.

The second sub-area of education which produced a high level
of conflict was the campus control bill, House Bill 815. This bill
prohibited unauthorized persons from entering upon school property,
the carrying of weapons in or upon school property, and the malicious
destruction of school property. The bill's subject and the timing of
its consideration, following disturbances at Lincoln University and
the events following Martin Luther King's death in the Spring of
1968, suggest that its intent might have been partially related to

racial concerns. Black legislators appeared to be more sensitive about the bill's purpose and its provisions than their urban non-black Democrat colleagues. Representative Holliday wrote:

> In an effort to show the House how ridiculous the bill was, I offered an amendment that all persons violating the bill be shot on sight, and the shooter held guiltless at law and be paid an appropriate bounty. The interesting thing about this amendment was that there were a few people in the House who took it seriously and really believed that loud-mouthed kids ought to be shot.[9]

As the orientation of Negro legislators seemed to be different on education issues, it is also possible to note a difference in two other areas with higher than average conflict. Taxation issues which produced higher levels of conflict focused on provisions for increasing the state income tax, permitting a local sales tax and raising the earnings tax in Kansas City. It is no surprise that those who represent persons occupying the lower positions on an economic scale would be more sensitive to increased tax burdens on their constituents. This should be particularly true at the state level of government, where taxation is commonly regarded as regressive, placing a disproportionate burden on those who are least capable of paying the cost of government. An illustration of black legislators' attitudes toward taxation issues can be seen by the following remarks on the income tax proposal.

> I was among those who were opposed to the increased proposal for persons with low incomes. I proposed an amendment which would leave the tax rate of those earning $2000 net income or less the same as it is at present. I was happy to see that all of the Black legislators in the House with one exception, supported my amendment. Nevertheless, the amendment lost by three votes. We are still hopeful, however, that before this House agrees upon a tax bill, that it will not require poor people to bear an unreasonable share of the tax burden.[10]

Included in public interest legislation were a number of issues which could be regarded as having an effect on the general citizenry. A higher degree of conflict between black and non-black urban Democrats existed in this area on questions related to interest rates on loans, the motor vehicle inspection law and provisions for hardship drivers licenses. Of those roll calls which showed the greatest level of dissimilarity between the two racial groups of urban Democrats, the votes on loan interest rates were the most conspicuous. Returning to the now stale topic of poverty, the differences in orientation can be captured in the following reported recommendation to Governor Warren E. Hearnes, by a Negro representative:

> Declaring that Senate Bill Number 175 /Increase in small loan rates7 is unfair, regressive and special interest in design, Representative Franklin Payne. . .recommended to Governor

Warren E. Hearnes /that he/. . .veto the proposed legislation on the basis it exploits the poor.

. . .providing more for the greedy and less for the needy is not the best interest of the state of Missouri, Payne said, 'I cannot see the righteousness of the state giving the small loan companies a bigger club to victimize the poor.'[11]

When inter-group conflict was present, the basic cause, as illustrated in the preceding paragraphs, was the economic and social orientation of the respective constituencies of the urban Democrat legislators.

In essence, it was those issues related to crime and poverty, both acknowledged as factors proportionately predominant in the black community, which had a tendency to produce orientations in the Negro legislator that resulted in different behavior patterns from his white urban party colleague. Although race itself was not found to be an overt feature of the conflict which did exist, the general position occupied by blacks in the societal system makes it difficult to distinguish between skin color and economic plight as the true source of voting differences.

Voting cohesion on black-sponsored legislation

If there is any validity to the assumptions that racial consciousness or constituency similarity are important factors in legislative behavior,[12] it is expected that Negro legislators would act in unison when voting on legislation sponsored by one of their number.

Thirty-one roll-call votes on Negro-sponsored legislation were recorded during the 1969 session.[13] These votes were taken on twenty-one different bills. By using the Rice Index of Cohesion to test group unity on those votes, a pattern of strong agreement appeared among the Negro House members when they had the opportunity to vote on bills sponsored by their black colleagues. The average Cohesion Index for the thirty-one votes was 91.0. Perhaps more revealing was the finding that they were in complete unison on twenty-five of the thirty-one votes. The Cohesion score dropped below 50.0 on only two roll calls. On the six bills where some division did occur, five votes showed the majority of the black delegation giving support to the sponsoring representative. On only one roll call did the majority of the black legislators oppose legislation sponsored by a black colleague. This vote was taken on the third reading of H.B. 758 entitled "Voter registration drives to be held at least three times a year in counties having board of election commissioners."

Since the Negro representatives in Missouri resided in two different cities, a logical question might be raised concerning the geographical factor in roll calls related to black-sponsored legislation where the black delegation was not completely cohesive. Only one roll-call vote produced a pattern of geographical differences. The bill was essentially local in nature in that it applied to public housing in St. Louis. The division among the black members came on the third reading of the bill when geographical differences seemed to play a dominant role, as the Kansas City representatives voted against the bill in unison, while their St. Louis counterparts unanimously supported it.

By categorizing the roll-call votes according to the topical nature of the bill being considered, cohesion within substantive legislative areas can be located. Civil rights and labor legislation produced the highest levels of cohesion, as shown by Table 7.3.

TABLE 7.3

COHESION SCORES[a] FOR BLACK REPRESENTATIVES ON ROLL CALLS
RELATED TO BLACK-SPONSORED LEGISLATION,
BY ISSUE CATEGORIES

Legislative Issue Category	Number of Roll Calls	Average Cohesion Scores
Civil Rights	9	100.0
Labor	2	100.0
State and Local Government	6	92.6
Law Enforcement	5	90.8
Elections	6	85.9
Public Housing	3	83.3
Total	31	91.0

[a]See Table 7.1 for explanation of cohesion scores.

Source: State of Missouri, House Journal, 75th General Assembly, Volume 1, Regular session, compiled by James C. Kirkpatrick, Secretary of State.

Black legislators and their political party on roll-call voting

Although not the complete explanation, there is no factor which "is likely to explain voting alignments more often or more fully than the party membership of legislators."[14] In the Missouri House the black representatives account for a small, but significant, portion (12%) of the Democratic Party membership. From these premises,

114

it is relevant to inquire into the relationship which existed between the black legislators and their political party in roll-call voting. In essence, did the black sub-group of the party deviate from the party's roll-call voting pattern?

On the 213 roll calls sampled, a majority of the black delegation opposed a majority of the non-black Democrats on forty-two votes. This represented a deviation from the party's norm on nearly 20 percent of the roll calls. Lacking in this figure, however, is the partisan importance of those votes. This void was rectified by examining the roll-call sample to locate votes on which a majority of the Democrats opposed a majority of the Republican membership. One hundred and eight such roll calls were found. On these partisan votes, the majority of the black delegation deviated from the party position on only fourteen roll calls (13%).

Although these statistics suggest that the Negro membership usually followed the party pattern in casting their votes, it is not sufficient evidence for a solid conclusion. A better method for examining inter-group conflict is the Index of Likeness. By using this device it was possible to show those roll calls which produced high levels of conflict between the political parties, as well as levels of conflict between the Negroes and other members of the Democratic Party. Its greatest asset is that it can demonstrate inter-group conflict which cannot be found by singling out only those votes where a majority of blacks oppose a majority of non-blacks.

If the 1969 session of the Missouri House is a fair example of Negro partisan voting behavior, it can be concluded that Negro legislators usually do not deviate greatly from the voting patterns of their party. When high levels of inter-party conflict occurred on roll calls, the differences between black and other Democrats was relatively low, as is shown in Table 7.4. Although the degree of dissimilarity between white and black Democrats was only minimal, it was more likely to occur on votes which did not stimulate high levels of inter-party conflict. This point can be demonstrated more clearly be condensing the information in Table 7.4 into a four-fold table showing high and low degrees of inter-group conflict for partisanship and racial factors within the Democratic Party, as shown by Table 7.5. Generally, the higher the degree of inter-party conflict, the lower the probability that Negroes would deviate from the party's voting pattern. Black Democrats tend to follow the party line in legislative voting when the party needs its support the most.

TABLE 7.4

A COMPARISON OF DEMOCRAT-REPUBLICAN AND BLACK-WHITE DEMOCRAT
CONFLICT ON ROLL CALLS BY USING THE INDEX OF LIKENESS[a]

| | Black-White Democrat Scores on the Index of Likeness[b] | | | | | | | | | | |
Democrat-Republican Scores on the Index of Likeness[b]	0 - 9.9	10.0- 19.9	20.0- 29.9	30.0- 39.9	40.0- 49.9	50.0- 59.9	60.0- 69.9	70.0- 79.9	80.0- 89.9	90.0- 100	Total Roll Calls
0 - 9.9	0	0	0	0	0	0	0	0	0	11	11
10.0-19.9	0	0	0	0	0	0	1	2	1	5	9
20.0-29.9	0	0	0	0	0	0	1	3	5	7	16
30.0-39.9	0	0	1	0	0	0	0	2	6	6	15
40.0-49.9	0	0	1	0	0	0	5	3	7	6	22
50.0-59.9	0	0	0	0	2	1	2	1	4	8	18
60.0-69.9	0	0	0	1	0	1	4	2	9	11	28
70.0-79.9	0	1	0	0	2	1	2	12	9	9	36
80.0-89.9	0	2	3	2	2	1	0	6	6	8	20
90.0-100	0	0	0	0	2	1	2	2	15	6	28
Total Roll Calls	0	3	5	3	8	5	17	33	62	77	213

[a]See Table 7.2 for explanation on Index of Likeness formula

TABLE 7.4 (Continued)

_____

- -

[b]The scores on the Index of Likeness vary from 0 to 100; with the former representing voting dissimilarity or conflict and the latter representing voting similarity or the lack of conflict.

Source: State of Missouri, House Journal, 75th General Assembly, Volume 1, Regular session, compiled by James C. Kirkpatrick, Secretary of State.

TABLE 7.5

A CONDENSED COMPARISON OF DEMOCRAT-REPUBLICAN AND BLACK-WHITE DEMOCRAT CONFLICT ON ROLL CALLS BASED UPON THE INDEX OF LIKENESS SCORES[a]

_____

- -

Black-White Democrat

	High degree of conflict	Low degree of conflict	
Democrat-Republican High degree of conflict	2 (1%)	71 (33%)	73 (34%)
Low degree of conflict	17 (8%)	123 (58%)	140 (66%)
	19 (9%)	194 (91%)	213 (100%)

_____

[a]See Table 7.4 for clarification.

Note: The four-fold table was devised by dividing the data in Table 7.4 into quartiles along the lines representing Index of Likeness scores of 50.0, the median point on the Index.

Source: State of Missouri, House Journal, 75th General Assembly, Volume 1, Regular session, compiled by James C. Kirkpatrick, Secretary of State.

The Impact of Black Cohesion on
Legislative Outputs

Thirteen members commonly do not represent a significant power-bloc in a body of 163 persons. As a small minority, Negro solons in the Missouri House are likely to have little, if any, impact on the results of policy decisions made by the lower chamber. The limitations on the group size of the Negro representatives, however, do not exclude them completely from a position of potential power. It is the manner by which the group utilizes its limited resources which will dictate its impact on legislative decisions.

Carmichael and Hamilton argued that the black community had to establish its own power base before it could become a viable political power.[15] This strategy of the independent power base suggests that Negro members of the legislative community would organize themselves into a group in order to maximize their influence over policy decisions.[16] From this vantage point, three questions need to be answered concerning the Negro strategy in the Missouri House during the 1969 session. First, did the Negro members feel that they should organize themselves into a cohesive bloc? Secondly, did they organize such a group? Thirdly, did they have the opportunities to utilize their power resources as a group in affecting the output of the House?

With only one exception, the Negro House delegation for the 75th General Assembly agreed that some effort should have been made to form a reference group among their membership. The membership differed, however, on the role such a group should perform. The alternative group roles can be specified as: (1) the establishment of a common legislative program, (2) the establishment of group unity on all legislative issues, (3) the establishment of group unity on all legislative issues which relate to the black community, (4) the establishment of group unity on controversial issues where their votes could serve as the balance of power, (5) the use of the group as a reference resource where the individual members communicate information on issues related to their committee assignments or areas of specialization to the full group.

Although the desire for the formation of a black caucus was present, it did not materialize during the 1969-70 session. Several veteran black legislators referred to the unity and cohesiveness of the group in 1969 as being at its lowest ebb in their tenure. Three explanations for the failure of black unity can be offered. First, the black political organization in Kansas City, Freedom Incorporated, did not support the incumbent Democrat governor, Warren E. Hearnes, who was re-elected in the 1968 elections. St. Louis representatives feared that their cross-state colleagues would use the caucus as a club to further their feud with the governor. Since they supported the governor, they did not want to weaken their relationship by an alliance with the party deviates. Naturally, it was the patronage benefits and rewards controlled by the governor which provided the foundation for their attitudes.

The second explanation results from dissension between various black political groups in St. Louis. In 1968 the first black congressman from Missouri was elected from a new district in St. Louis. Three blacks sought the party's nomination in the Democratic primary. State legislator Troupe and the husband of State Representative Calloway were two of the candidates. The third black candidate, William Clay, emerged as the eventual victor. Although Troupe withdrew from the race prior to the election, fearing that a fourth candidate, a white, would be successful with the division of black votes, the multi-member contest resulted in cutting deep cleavages among the black political leadership in St. Louis. The wounds had not healed when the legislature met in 1969, and an atmosphere of distrust and disunity prevailed among the members of the St. Louis delegation.

The final explanation can be viewed as a corollary of the first two. It is simply the lack of coordination and centralization of black political leadership in the state. Not only is state-wide leadership absent, there is also a void in unified leadership within both of the metropolitan areas of the state. Whereas Freedom Incorporated has succeeded in controlling three of the four black representatives from Kansas City, no concentrated effort has been successful in bringing the various ward organizations in St. Louis together in a larger political association.

In answering the first two questions the third may have become moot and irrelevant. It is apparent that the failure to organize a cohesive group probably resulted in weakening the black membership as a power source in the legislature. The question, however, remains important. Its importance rests upon the impact a cohesive group might have had if it had existed.[17] In other words, had the black members of the House been unified could they have influenced legislative outputs?

The black House members can be described as having had the potential of influence over legislative policy output when a variation in their voting patterns would have resulted in a different decision. More precisely, influence potential can be said to have existed in situations where (1) withdrawal of some of all black support from the prevailing side would have altered the decision, and where (2) the Negroes would have altered the House's action by casting some or all of their votes for the nonprevailing position. These two conditions cover all three possible roll-call situations: those where a simple majority of the present members determine the fate of legislative action; those where a constitutional majority is required for an affirmative decision; and those where extraordinary constitutional majority (two thirds of the House membership) is required for a favorable verdict.

As was noted earlier, high degrees of conflict in voting behavior were uncommon. The outcome of 140 from the total of 1,047 roll calls (13.4%) could have been altered with position changes by thirteen or fewer legislators. From this sample of vulnerable roll calls, where a small group of legislators could have changed the legislative product, the black representatives could have provided the balance of power on eighty-six votes. This represents 61 percent of the vulnerable roll calls and 8 percent of all the recorded roll calls.

The impact of Negro assemblymen on policy determinations can be labeled as negligible when considering the total number of roll calls. Their influence potential on vulnerable votes, however, could have provided them with a power resource if they had acted in a concerted manner. Had the black legislators sought a bargaining lever for their own legislative programs or for legislative outputs beneficial to their constituencies, their position as a power force could have been maximized on vulnerable roll calls where their votes would have provided the balance of power.

Of the ten Negro legislators who responded to an inquiry on the use of group bloc voting as a legitimate resource on controversial issues, eight agreed that the black delegation could have had an impact on the legislative product. More important, however, is the question, did the Negro representatives as a group act in a manner which maximized their potential influence on those vulnerable roll calls? Since the Negroes were not successful in forming a unified reference group in 1969, their behavior was not overtly evident on these votes.

Nonetheless, by analyzing the voting patterns of the Negro group some understanding of their ability to maximize their power on the vulnerable roll calls can be found. The average score for the black representatives on the Index of Cohesion for these eighty-six roll calls was 68.1. This does not represent as high a level of black group cohesion as was found on other roll calls, particularly those votes taken on legislative issues sponsored by Negroes, where their score was 91.0. As a group the blacks were perfectly cohesive on only thirty-two of the eighty-six roll calls (37%) where they had a potential influence. A further indication of their failure to maximize the potential impact can be demonstrated by the fact that on only five of these roll calls did all thirteen members vote and vote alike on the issue.

Had the black legislators made an effort to maximize their role as the "balance of power" on vulnerable roll calls higher cohesion scores would have been expected. It can be concluded that the blacks, during the 1969 session, did not utilize their position as a potential influence to the extent which would have provided the utmost impact on policy decisions. When a group's votes are divided or are not voted, the potential influence for the group is weakened.

Black Absenteeism

From the premise that a solon in a representative democracy
is to cast his constituents' vote in the legislative process, it is
assumed that one of the rudimentary purposes for his existence is
the answering of roll-call votes. While legislators do much more
than simply answer the ringing of the bell when votes are to be
taken, their presence on recorded roll calls can provide some understanding of his performance as a representative. James Q. Wilson's
report on two black Congressmen, Adam Clayton Powell and William
Dawson, noted their rather high rate of absenteeism on roll-call
votes.[18] Although this pattern of behavior was not then regarded as
related to their race, its occurrence did raise a question about
these black legislators. The Negro assemblyman, like any other,
will occasionally have justifiable reasons for missing a roll call.
The vote might be on an issue which is irrelevant to the concerns of
his constituency. Or he might be occupied with business, either
private (since he is a part-time public official in Missouri as in
most other states), or public (those other responsibilities related
to his position as a public official, such as the performance of
errand-running duties for his constituency). It is, however, doubtful
that the black legislator would have reason to legitimately miss
roll-call votes more often than any other legislator.

During the regular session of the 75th Missouri General
Assembly, the black legislative delegation had a higher proportion
of absenteeism on roll calls than did the total membership of the
House.[19] For the 1,047 roll-call votes recorded during this period,
the average attendance for the total House membership was 88 percent.
The non-black membership of the lower chamber averaged slightly
higher with 89 percent attendance on roll calls. And as can be
deducted from those statistics, the black membership of the House
averaged somewhat less, 78 percent attendance on a roll call. For
the Negroes this meant that on an average roll-call vote nearly
three of the thirteen members were recorded as absent. The total
black delegation in the House managed to answer less than 10 percent
of the total number of votes, as shown in Table 7.6. Regional
influence as a possible explanation for this absenteeism rate can
be dismissed by comparing the black rates with that of non-black
urban legislators (87 percent).

In seeking a cause for the relatively high absentee rate
among the Negro members of the Missouri House, roll calls on legislative
issues sponsored by members of the black delegation were isolated
for examination. Since these issues were authored by blacks, it
seems that a valid assumption could be made that these issues
represented policy areas with above average importance to the Negro
legislator's constituency. If this assumption is valid, it is
expected that the absenteeism rate would descend when comparing the
rates for all roll calls and those roll calls on legislative items
sponsored by blacks. This conclusion is substantiated in Figure 7.1.

TABLE 7.6

BLACK ABSENTEEISM ON RECORDED ROLL CALLS[a]

Number of Black Representatives Absent on Roll Call	Number of Roll Calls	Percentage[b]
0	98	9%
1	225	21%
2	199	19%
3	172	16%
4	151	14%
5	94	9%
6	43	4%
7	19	2%
8	31	3%
9	6	1%
10	8	1%
11	1	**
12	0	0
13	0	0
	1,047	99%

[a]Absenteeism is defined as not being recorded as either "aye" or "no" or "present but not voting" on a roll call.

[b]Percentages were rounded.

**less than one per cent.

Source: State of Missouri, House Journal, 75th General Assembly, Volume 1, Regular session, compiled by James C. Kirkpatrick, Secretary of State.

FIGURE 7.1

A COMPARISON OF BLACK ABSENTEEISM[a] ON ROLL CALLS
RELATED TO BLACK-SPONSORED LEGISLATION

Percent of Group Members Answering Roll Calls	All Roll Calls	Roll Calls Related to Black-Sponsored Legislation
89%	A	
88%	B	
87%	C	
86%		
85%		
84%		
83%		
82%		
81%		
80%		
79%		
78%	D	

A = Non-black House members
B = All House members
C = Non-black urban House members
D = Black House members

[a]Absenteeism is defined as not voting either "aye," "no," or "present but not voting."

Source: State of Missouri, House Journal, 75th General Assembly, Volume 1, Regular session, compiled by James C. Kirkpatrick, Secretary of State.

Although the direction of Negro absenteeism fulfilled the expectation, it did not surpass the attendance proportion of the remaining membership. It thus can be stated that black representatives are more likely to cast a vote on issues pertinent to their constituency but are still less likely to ballot than other members of the legislature.

Factors promoting this phenomenon remain unknown. Several explanations can be offered, none of which, however, can be substantiated as the correct influence. First, the primary source of income to the black legislator may demand more attention than is true of his colleagues. The black representative does not hold an economic position which permits complete independence when the legislature is in session. He is either dependent upon someone else for his employment, which commonly means that he must perform his task to keep his job, or he operates a relatively small business, which requires him to divide his attention during the legislative session. Secondly, the psychological impact of repression and subordination of the Negro may remain as a sense of alienation, even though he has managed to become a part of the establishment. Thirdly, he may have been frustrated by his lack of effectiveness in the legislative process.

Summary

Consideration of legislative roll-call participation of the black representatives in the Missouri House was oriented toward group behavior, rather than individual behavior. Roll-call participation was discussed by examining three separate concerns. First were the roll-call voting patterns of the black delegation. The information in this section was based primarily on 213 roll calls selected for analysis. These roll calls were selected on the basis of their relevance to the urban areas of the state, from those roll calls which exhibited some degree of conflict among the House membership. Roll calls illustrating conflict were defined as those where more than 10 percent of the House membership opposed the prevailing majority. Those roll calls were analyzed by using the Indexes of Cohesion and Likeness devised by Stuart Rice. In order to determine the significance of black voting patterns, the voting patterns of other legislative groups, when appropriate, were used for comparison.

Several conclusions were drawn from the inquiry into voting patterns. First, the black legislators demonstrated a high level of cohesion on roll-call voting. Generally, this was not a unique pattern when comparing their cohesion to that of non-black urban Democrats. The black legislators, however, were more cohesive in the legislative areas of civil rights and law enforcement than their non-black urban Democrat counterparts. Secondly, legislative roll calls did not, generally, demonstrate dissimilar voting patterns between black and non-black urban Democrat legislators. The highest levels of conflict between these two groups occurred on issues related to education and law enforcement. The differences in constituencies and race orientations might provide, at least, a partial explanation for those differences. Thirdly, the black solons were strongly unified on roll-call votes taken on legislative items sponsored by members of the Negro delegation. Fourthly, the Negro representatives only rarely deviated from the roll-call patterns of the Democratic Party. Where partisan conflict occurred, a dissimilar pattern of voting between the Republicans and Democrats, the black sub-group of the Democratic Party supported the party's position.

The second concern was the black legislators' impact on legislative output. As a group the Negro representatives perceived the concept of a black caucus as being beneficial to their effectiveness in affecting legislative output. During the 1969 session, however, there was no formal structure for such a legislative sub-group. As a result, no formal element existed which could coordinate the group's voting behavior. A coordinated group effort by the blacks could have been vital as the balance of power to legislative output on a limited number of roll calls (8%). There was no evidence to support a conclusion that the Negro representatives were acting as a unified group on these roll calls where the outcome was vulnerable to such a group effort.

Absenteeism was the third concern. Based on the premise that voting on roll calls is an indicator of a legislator's participation in the legislative process, the data showed that black assemblymen had lower attendance records. Information for the Missouri House in 1969 demonstrated that black members participated less often on roll-call votes than did non-black members of the House.

Notes

[1]State of Missouri, House Journal, 75th General Assembly, Volume 1, Regular session, compiled by James C. Kirkpatrick, Secretary of State.

[2]For an explanation on the Rice Index of Cohesion see Lee F. Anderson, Meredith W. Watts, and Allen R. Wilcox, Legislative Roll-Call Analysis (Evanston: Northwestern University Press, 1966), pp. 32-35; Duncan MacRae, Jr., Issues and Parties in Legislative Voting: Methods of Statistical Analysis (New York: Harper and Row, 1970), p. 179; and Ralph K. Juitt and Robert L. Peabody, Congress: Two Decades of Analysis (New York: Harper and Row, 1969), p. 47. The Index was originally proposed in Stuart Rice, Quantitative Methods in Politics (New York: Alfred A. Knopf, 1928), chapter 15.

[3]$$\frac{\text{"Aye" votes} - \text{"No" votes}}{\text{"Aye" votes} + \text{"No" votes}} \times 100.0 = \text{Index of Cohesion}$$

[4]The Index of Likeness is discussed in Anderson, et al., op. cit., pp. 44-45, and by its originator Rice, op. cit., chapter 15.

[5]The formula may be stated as:
    100- (% of Group A voting "Aye" - % of Group B voting
    "Aye") = Index of Likeness.

[6]Representative Harold L. Holliday, "The Legislative Scene,"
Kansas City Call, June 6-12, 1969, p. 5.

[7]Representative Harold L. Holliday, "The Legislative Scene,"
Kansas City Call, June 27-July 3, 1969, p. 2.

[8]Representative Harold L. Holliday, "The Legislative Scene,"
Kansas City Call, April 25-May 1, 1969, p. 2.

[9]Representative Harold L. Holliday, "The Legislative Scene,"
Kansas City Call, June 13-19, 1969, p. 2.

[10]Representative Harold L. Holliday, "The Legislative Scene,"
Kansas City Call, March 28-April 3, 1969, p. 3.

[11]"Representative Payne Asks Governor to Veto Small Loan Interest
Increase," St. Louis Argus, July 18, 1969, p. 1, 11A. The entire
letter was printed in the St. Louis American, July 17, 1969, p. 6.

[12]For a discussion on constituency similarity and shared attitudes
toward public policy see Lewis A. Froman, Jr., Congressmen and Their
Constituencies (Chicago: Rand McNally and Company, 1963), pp. 11-14.

[13]State of Missouri, House Journal, 75th General Assembly, Volume
1, Regular session, compiled by James C. Kirkpatrick, Secretary of
State.

[14]Malcolm E. Jewell, The State Legislature (2nd ed.; New York:
Random House, 1969), p. 107.

[15]Stokely Carmichael and Charles V. Hamilton, Black Power: The
Politics of Liberation in America (New York: Vintage Books, Inc.,
1967), pp. 58-84.

[16]For a discussion on this point see James Q. Wilson, "The Negro
in Politics," Daedalus, XCIV (Fall, 1965), 949-973. Reprinted in
Lawrence H. Fuchs, ed., American Ethnic Politics (New York: Harper
and Row, Publishers, 1968), pp. 217-246.

[17]For a discussion on cohesive voting behavior as a mechanism of
political influence see William R. Keech, The Impact of Negro Voting
(Chicago: Rand McNally and Company, 1968), p. 8.

[18]James Q. Wilson, "Two Negro Politicians: An Interpretation,"
Midwest Journal of Political Science, IV (November, 1960), 346-369.

[19]Absenteeism is defined as not being recorded as either "aye,"
"no," or "present but not voting" on a roll call.

CHAPTER VIII

CONCLUSION

The differentiation of individuals and groups in the American society on the criteria of skin color has been well documented. This differentiation has not been limited to social interaction and behavior, it has also been traditional in the political aspects of life. It was hypothesized in the introduction that racial character- istics would be important in the legislative system. Any suppositions to the contrary can be dismissed from the discussion in this manuscript. Assimilation of blacks into the political realm has not occurred to the point where ascribed racial characteristics are meaningless.

The research reported in this study demonstrates that race remains an important variable in the Missouri House of Representatives. This conclusion can be supported by several components of this study. (1) All of the black House members represented constituencies which shared their racial heritage. Since their constituencies were predominantly Negro (89.2%) the black lawmakers were cognizant of racial differentiation. (2) The racial make-up of the black solons' constituencies resulted in an orientation reflective of racial distinctions. The black representatives introduced several legislative items which were directed at eliminating racial distinctions or dis- crimination and several bills which promoted and benefited the cause of Negroes. Many of these bills were concerned with social and economic problems which affect all persons in the society, but where the major impact of the legislative program would be perceived as being in the black community. (3) Political interest and career aspirations and expectations of the black legislators were based upon racial considerations. Several entered political life as a result of racial concerns and activities. The desire for a political future was dependent upon factors related to race, basically a black constituency. (4) The participation and cohesion of black legislators on roll-call voting was greater when the roll call was taken on a motion pertaining to a legislative bill introduced by a black colleague than on other votes. (5) Even though the black House members did not organize a formal sub-group of the legislature on a racial basis during the 1969-70 session, there was a desire among the Negro solons for such a group. A black caucus was perceived as being important to the effectiveness of blacks in achieving favorable attention and outputs for blacks from the legislative system.

Within the legislative structures and processes, the black representatives in Missouri were confronted with racial differentiation. When compared to their non-black colleagues, the black assemblymen in the House were less powerful, influential, and successful. This second conclusion was based upon data which consistently produced patterns showing blacks relegated to secondary roles and less able to achieve desired goals. No Negro House member was selected for a primary leadership position. The only leadership roles that blacks were assigned to perform were committee roles. Of the forty standing committees, blacks chaired two and served as vice-chairman of seven committees. A review of the committees in the House exhibited that these committees, however, were not committees of any significant importance in the conduction of the lower chamber's business. As in the performance of leadership roles, Negro lawmakers also were not assigned to the most active and important standing committees. Differentiation or differences between black and non-black House members in securing policies which they initiated was also found. Black legislators were less likely to achieve passage of their sponsored legislation and were more likely to see their bills defeated or given their legislative death in the committee system than were non-black representatives. The failure of black-sponsored legislation to receive favorable standing committee action increased as the importance (leadership roles) and the presence of fellow black colleagues on the committee declined.

One of the purposes of this research was the acquisition of information which would serve as a basis for the characterization of Negro solons. Black legislators were found to be both similar and dissimilar to their non-black peers in the Missouri House in 1969-70 and to those generalizations found in earlier studies of legislators. Similar to other legislators, black legislators had resided in the area of their districts for the major portion of their lives, came from the same general age category, received their initial political orientation at an early age by participating in political campaigns, had pre-legislative experiences in the political party organizations, and were politically ambitious. Black members of the Missouri lower chamber were also found to be moderates rather than militants, especially in their race attitudes where they emphasized welfare goals and favored non-violent and orderly protest and negotiation to violence as a mechanism for the solution of racial problems. Like other legislators, the black lawmakers sponsored legislation which was oriented to the correction of problems in the constituencies they represented. In the Missouri House the black solons were found to be highly cohesive on roll-call votes, but this was not unique since other urban Democrats were as cohesive. It was also demonstrated that the voting patterns of white and black urban Democrats in the House were similar. Lastly, the black legislators were strong party supporters on roll calls, especially when the differences between Republicans and Democrats were the greatest.

The characteristics exhibited by Negro solons were commonly similar to expected patterns. Deviations from the norm or expected patterns were found in only a few situations. There were some atypical patterns found in examining the social-economic characteristics of the black legislators. Their education was different in that they lacked the level of academic training in institutions of higher learning. The educational pattern of blacks was comparable to non-blacks only when the black educational achievements in vocational and technical training were included. Similar to the educational patterns, occupational patterns differed for the blacks and non-blacks. Blacks lacked the professional occupations demonstrated by non-blacks. Instead of coming from professional or business occupations, as is common for state legislators, blacks came from business or white-collar occupations. Differences in social class categorization was found for both the family background and the positions currently held by the black lawmakers as compared to the general patterns described in other studies. Even though the findings in this research showed the blacks as different in educational achievements, occupations, and social class, there is an expectation that the black legislator, like his non-black colleagues, is atypical of his constituents by having more education, a more prestigious occupation, and a higher social class position. The election of black representatives also showed a deviating pattern. The Democratic Party was considerably stronger in black legislative districts than in other urban districts electing Democrats. Finally, it was also found that black House members were less likely to participate in the legislative roll-call voting process than were non-black legislators.

It was thought that when the proportion of a sub-group grows within a larger group, its power and influence would also increase. With the three-fold increase in black representation in the 1960's it was expected that blacks would have obtained a position of some influence and power in the Missouri House. There has been no evidence in this research which suggests that blacks have become a source of power in the House. It is necessary to make a distinction between the potential of influence and the exercise of such influence. It was demonstrated that on a limited number of roll-call votes the black House membership could have altered the decision made by the House. These votes provided a basis for potential influence in the legislative processes. A strategy properly utilized on these votes could have placed the blacks in a position of deciding the outcome of the vote, thus making it possible that other groups or individuals in the House would be willing to accommodate black legislative desires in order to accomplish their own. It is a simple expectation of log-rolling. In order to perform such a role in the legislature a sub-group must first form a cohesive group so as to maximize its influence. This the blacks did not manage in the regular session of the 1969-70 General Assembly. The blacks did perceive such a cohesive reference group as desirable and beneficial to the concerns of the black community. Political considerations of the black solons seemed to deny them an opportunity for such influence.

Conclusions drawn from this study are applicable only to the Missouri House for the 1969-70 session. It is expected that some of these findings might be altered should other legislatures be examined. As an initial examination of black lawmakers, the conclusions reported in the preceding pages should provide springboards for

future studies of Negro legislators. In summary, from this project
it was found that the black legislators were cognizant of race in
the performance of their legislative responsibilities, that they
had not been assimilated thoroughly into the legislative institutions,
and that they were not, as blacks, a cohesive source of power or
influence in the legislature.

BIBLIOGRAPHY

Books

Almond, Gabriel A., and G. Bingham Powell, Jr. Comparative Politics: A Developmental Approach. Boston: Little, Brown and Company, 1966.

Anderson, Lee F., Meredith W. Watts, Jr., and Allen R. Wilcox. Legislative Roll-Call Analysis. Evanston: Northwestern University Press, 1966.

Baker, Gordon E. The Reapportionment Revolution. New York: Random House, Inc., 1966.

Banfield, Edward C. Big City Politics. New York: Random House, Inc., 1963.

_____, and James Q. Wilson. City Politics. New York: Random House, Inc., 1963.

Barber, James David. The Lawmakers. New Haven: Yale University Press, 1965.

Bentley, Arthur. The Process of Government. Chicago: University of Chicago Press, 1908.

Brewer, J. Mason. Negro Legislators of Texas. New York: Jenkins Publishing Company, 1970.

Buchanan, William. Legislative Partisanship: The Deviant Case of California. Berkeley: University of California Press, 1963.

Bullock, Charles S., III, and Harrell R. Rogers, Jr. (eds.). Black Political Attitudes. Chicago: Markham Publishing Company, 1972.

Burgess, Elaine. Negro Leadership in a Southern City. Chapel Hill: The University of North Carolina Press, 1960.

Campbell, Angus, Philip E. Converse, Warren E. Miller, and Donald E. Stokes. The American Voter. New York: John Wiley and Sons, Inc., 1960.

Carmichael, Stokely, and Charles V. Hamilton. <u>Black Power: The Politics of Liberation in America</u>. New York: Vintage Books, 1967.

Clark, Kenneth. <u>Dark Ghetto</u>. New York: Harper and Row, 1967.

_____, Julian Bond, and Richard G. Hatcher. <u>The Black Man in American Politics</u>. Washington, D.C.: Metropolitan Applied Research Center, Inc., 1969.

Crane, Wilder, Jr., and Meredith W. Watts, Jr. <u>State Legislative Systems</u>. Englewood Cliffs, N.J.: Prentice-Hall, Inc., 1968.

Dahl, Robert A. <u>Who Governs? Democracy and Power in an American City</u>. New Haven: Yale University Press, 1961.

David, Paul T., and Ralph Eisenberry. <u>State Legislative Districting</u>. Chicago: Public Administration Service, 1962.

Drake, St. Clair, and Horace Cayton. <u>Black Metropolis</u>. New York: Harcourt, Brace and World, Inc., 1965.

Dymally, Mervyn M. (ed.). <u>The Black Politician: His Struggle for Power</u>. Belmont, Calif.: Duxburg Press, 1971.

Easton, David. <u>A Framework for Political Analysis</u>. Englewood Cliffs, N.J.: Prentice-Hall, Inc., 1965.

Easton, David. <u>The Political System</u>. New York: Alfred A. Knopf, Inc., 1953.

Epstein, Leon D. <u>Politics in Wisconsin</u>. Madison: The University of Wisconsin Press, 1958.

Fiellin, Alan. "The Functions of Informal Groups: A State Delegation," <u>New Perspectives on the House of Representatives</u>. Robert L. Peabody and Nelson W. Polsby, eds.; Chicago: Rand McNally and Co., 1963.

Frazier, E. Franklin. <u>Black Bourgeoisie: The Rise of a New Middle Class</u>. New York: The Free Press, 1957.

Froman, Lewis A., Jr. <u>Congressmen and Their Constituencies</u>. Chicago: Rand McNally and Co., 1963.

Fuchs, Lawrence H. (ed.). <u>American Ethnic Politics</u>. New York: Harper and Row, Publishers, 1968.

Glazer, Nathan, and Daniel Patrick Moynihan. <u>Beyond the Melting Pot</u>. Cambridge, Mass.: The M.I.T. Press, 1963.

Gordon, Milton M. Assimilation in American Life. New York: Oxford
    University Press, 1964.

Gosnell, Harold F. Negro Politicians: The Rise of Negro Politicians
    in Chicago. Chicago: Phoenix Press, 1966.

Gray, Kenneth E. A Report on Politics in St. Louis. Cambridge, Mass.:
    Joint Center for Urban Studies, 1959. Mimeo.

Heard, Alexander (ed.). State Legislatures in American Politics.
    Englewood Cliffs, N.J.: Prentice-Hall, Inc., 1966.

Huitt, Ralph D., and Robert L. Peabody. Congress: Two Decades of
    Analysis. New York: Harper and Row, Publishers, 1969.

Hyman, Herbert H. "The Value Systems of Different Classes," Class,
    Status and Power. Reinhard Bendix and Seymour Martin Lipset,
    eds.; 2nd ed.; New York: The Free Press, 1966.

Jewell, Malcolm E. The State Legislature. 2nd ed.; New York: Random
    House, Inc., 1969.

_____, and Samuel C. Patterson. The Legislative Process in the
    United States. New York: Random House, Inc., 1966.

Karsch, Robert F. The Government of Missouri. 11th ed.; Columbia,
    Mo.: Lucas Brothers Publishers, 1971.

_____. The Standing Committees of the Missouri General Assembly.
    Columbia, Mo.: Bureau of Government Research of the
    University of Missouri, 1959.

Keech, William R. The Impact of Negro Voting. Chicago: Rand McNally
    and Company, 1968.

Keefe, William J., and Morris S. Ogul. The American Legislative Process.
    Englewood Cliffs, N.J.: Prentice-Hall, Inc., 1964.

Key, V. O., Jr. American State Politics: An Introduction. New York:
    Alfred A. Knopf, 1956.

Ladd, Everett Carll, Jr. Negro Political Leadership in the South.
    New York: Cornell University Press, 1966.

Lathan, Earl. The Group Basis of Politics. Ithaca, N.Y.: Cornell
    University Press, 1952.

Lee, Eugene C. The Presiding Officer and the Rules Committee in
    Legislatures of the United States. Berkeley: Bureau of Public
    Administration, University of California, 1952.

Leuthold, David A. The Missouri Legislature: A Preliminary Profile. Columbia, Mo.: Research Center of the School of Business and Public Administration, University of Missouri, 1967.

Lockard, Duane. New England State Politics. Princeton, N.J.: Princeton University Press, 1959.

MacRae, Duncan, Jr. Issues and Parties in Legislative Voting: Methods of Statistical Analysis. New York: Harper and Row, Publishers, 1970.

Matthews, Donald R., and James W. Prothro. Negroes and the New Southern Politics. New York: Harcourt, Brace and World, Inc., 1966.

Myrdal, Gunnar. An American Dilemma. 2nd ed.; New York: Harper and Row, 1962.

National Register of Black Elected Officials. Washington, D.C.: Metropolitan Applied Research Center, Inc., 1970.

Record, Wilson. The Negro and the Communist Party. Durham: University of North Carolina Press, 1951.

Revolution in Civil Rights. 3rd ed.; Washington, D.C.: Congressional Quarterly, Inc., 1967.

Rice, Stuart A. Quantitative Methods in Politics. New York: Alfred A. Knopf, 1928.

Shibutani, Tamotsu, and Kian M. Kwan. Ethnic Stratification. New York: Macmillan Company, 1965.

Silberman, Charles E. Crisis in Black and White. New York: Random House, Inc., 1964.

Sorauf, Frank J. Party Politics in America. Boston: Little, Brown and Company, 1968.

_____. Party and Representation: Legislative Politics in Pennsylvania. New York: Atherton Press, 1963.

Steiner, Gilbert Y., and Samuel K. Gove. Legislative Politics in Illinois. Urbana: University of Illinois Press, 1960.

Truman, David B. The Congressional Party. New York: John Wiley and Sons, Inc., 1959.

_____, The Governmental Process. New York: Alfred A. Knopf, 1951.

Wahlke, John, et al. The Legislative System. New York: John Wiley and Sons, Inc., 1962.

Walton, Hanes, Jr. Black Politics. New York: J. B. Lippincott
     Company, 1972.

_____, The Negro in Third Party Politics. Philadelphia:
     Dorrance and Company, 1969.

Wilson, James Q. Negro Politics: The Search for Leadership. New
     York: The Free Press, 1960.

Wilson, Woodrow. Congressional Government. New York: Meridian
     Books, 1956.

Articles

Aberbach, Joel, and Jack Walker. "The Meaning of Black Power: A
     Comparison of White and Black Interpretations of a Political
     Slogan," American Political Science Review. LXIV (June,
     1970), 367-388.

Axelrod, Robert. "Where the Votes Come From: An Analysis of
     Electoral Coalitions, 1952-1968," American Political Science
     Review. LXVI (March, 1972), 11-24.

Beth, Loren P., and William C. Harvard. "Committee Stacking and
     Political Power in Florida," Journal of Politics. XXIII
     (February, 1961), 57-83.

Derge, David R. "The Lawyer as Decision-Maker in the American State
     Legislature," Journal of Politics. XXI (August, 1959),
     426-431.

_____. "Metropolitan and Outstate Alignments in Illinois and
     Missouri Legislative Delegations," American Political
     Science Review. LII (December, 1958), 1051-1065.

Fenton, John H., and Kenneth W. Vines. "Negro Registration in
     Louisiana," American Political Science Review. LI
     (September, 1957), 104-713.

Fiellan, Alan. "The Functions of Informal Groups in Legislative
     Institutions," Journal of Politics. XXIV (February, 1962),
     72-91.

Franklin, John Hope. "The Two Worlds of Race: A Historical View,"
     Daedalus. XCIV (Fall, 1965), 899-920.

Gordon, Milton M. "Assimilation in America: Theory and Reality,"
     Daedalus. XC (Spring, 1961), 263-283.

Hadwiger, Don F. "Representations in the Missouri General Assembly," Missouri Law Review. XXIV (April, 1959), 178-195.

Holloway, Harry. "Negro Political Strategy: Coalition or Independent Power Politics," Social Science Quarterly. XLIX (December, 1968), 534-547.

Jewell, Malcolm E. "Party Voting in American State Legislatures," American Political Science Review. XLIX (September, 1956), 773-791.

Keefe, William J. "Comparative Study of the Role of Political Parties," Western Political Quarterly. IX (September, 1956), 726-742.

MacRae, Duncan, Jr. "The Relation Between Roll Call Votes and Constituencies in the Massachusetts House of Representatives," American Political Science Review. XLVI (December, 1952), 1046-1055.

_____, and Edith K. MacRae. "Legislators' Social Status and Their Votes," American Journal of Sociology. LXVI (May, 1961), 599-603.

Mann, Dean E. "The Legislative Committee System in Arizona," Western Political Quarterly. XIV (Decdmber, 1961), 925-941.

Matthews, Donald R., and James W. Prothro. "Social and Economic Factors and Negro Registration in the South," American Political Science Review. LVII (March, 1957), 24-44.

Parenti, Michael. "Ethnic Politics and the Persistence of Ethnic Identification," American Political Science Review. LXI (September, 1967), 460-472.

Russell, John C. "Racial Groups in the New Mexico Legislature," The Annals (January, 1938), pp. 62-71.

Selgiman, Lester G. "Political Recruitment and Party Structure," American Political Science Review. (March, 1961), 77-86.

Wilson, James Q. "The Negro in Politics," Daedalus. XCIV (Fall, 1965), 949-953.

_____. "Two Negro Politicians: An Interpretation," Midwest Journal of Political Science. IV (November, 1960), 346-369.

Wolfinger, Raymond E. "The Development and Persistance of Ethnic Voting," American Political Science Review. LIX (December, 1965), 896-908.

Government Documents

Election Laws of the State of Missouri, 1969-70. Jefferson City,
        Mo.: James C. Kirkpatrick, Secretary of State, N. D.

Official Manual State of Missouri, 1969-70. Jefferson City, Mo.:
        James C. Kirkpatrick, Secretary of State, 1970.

State of Missouri, House Journal. 75th General Assembly, I, Regular
        Session, Compiled by James C. Kirkpatrick, Secretary of State.

U.S. Bureau of Census, Census of Housing: 1970, Block Statistics.
        Final Report HC (3)-135 Kansas City, Mo.-Kans. Urbanized
        Area. Washington, D.C.: U.S. GOvernment Printing Office,
        1971.

U.S. Bureau of Census, Census of Housing: 1970, Block Statistics.
        Final Report HC (3)-137 St. Louis, Mo.-Ill. Urbanized
        Area. Washington, D.C.: U.S. Government Printing Office,
        1971.

Unpublished

Jones, Mack H. "Black Officeholders in Local Governments of the South"
        (unpublished paper presented at the Southern Political
        Science Association Meeting, November, 1970).

Young, George D. "The Role of Political Parties in the Missouri
        House of Representatives" (unpublished Ph.D. dissertation,
        University of Missouri, 1958).

Periodicals

The Black Politician (Summer, 1970).

Time (April 6, 1970).

Newspapers

Kansas City Call.

Kansas City Star.

St. Louis American.

St. Louis Argus.

St. Louis Post Dispatch.